Communicating with the

5 *Generations*

in the Workplace

Mary L. Erlain, Business Coach

Meredith "Kit" Bromfield, M.A.Ed.

Forward by: Elliot Richardson, Esq.
CEO, Small Business Advocacy Council

ISBN-10: 1495206688
ISBN-13: 978-1495206689

Printed in the United States of America

For permission to use material, contact:

Mary Erlain
M.Erlain@Peak-DS.com
(630) 768-1422

Meredith Bromfield
Meredith@MeredithBromfield.com
(630) 618-9400

Dedication

Mary:

I dedicate this book to my grandson, Noah, who brightens my life each day.

I give all the glory to my Lord and Savior in guiding my mind and my hands in the creation of this book.

Meredith:

I dedicate this book to the entire Memory Care Unit staff of Meadowbrook Manor in Bolingbrook for taking such good care of my mom, Helen. Thank you for giving me peace of mind knowing that my mom is in loving hands.

Mary and I also dedicate this book to our dear friend, Cynthia, who brought us together many years ago. We are so grateful to her for recognizing the possibilities of a great relationship in encouraging a divine encounter between Meredith and Mary.

Forward

"As CEO of the Small Business Advocacy Council (SBAC), I consistently hear about the challenges small business owners encounter when hiring, motivating, and retaining top talent. Indeed, because smaller businesses cannot always match the compensation or benefits offered by their larger counterparts, creating a positive culture at the workplace is critical for smaller companies. Having worked with hundreds of business professionals, Mary and Meredith understand the challenges associated with integrating today's diverse work force which often spans five generations. This book is a valuable resource for those business owners and supervisors struggling to transform a multi-generational work force into a cohesive and motivated team.

"Every employee has a story. They all have a world view that impacts the way they perform at the workplace. Mary and Meredith can give you the necessary tools to get the most out of your employees, regardless of the label we associate with their generation. I highly recommend this book to business owners, supervisors, parents, or anyone looking to communicate better with diverse individuals whose core values were formed during different times. Mary and Meredith will help you understand how to effectively communicate and motivate a multi-generational workforce. As we all know, a team must all row a boat in the same direction to succeed, regardless of the age of the folks on board. Enjoy this great book."

Elliot Richardson, Esq.
CEO, Small Business Advocacy Council (SBAC)

The SBAC is an organization providing small business owners, their employees, and those with whom they do business a voice in government. The SBAC also focuses on helping each member succeed through marketing and networking.

Partner, Korey, Cotter, Heather & Richardson, LLC. Elliot is a commercial litigation attorney where he represents business owners in commercial and business matters. He is also of counsel at Kralovoc, Jambois & Schwartz, a top medical malpractice and Plaintiffs law firm.

Praise for 5 Generations

"*10 Answer Keys, Communicating with the 5 Generations in the Workplace* is an insightful, detailed profile of different generational thinking with solutions to bring your team to its peak performance."

Linda Heyse-Highland, President
LinJen Promotions, Inc.
www.linjen.com

"Looking to boost productivity in your work force in 2014? *10 Answer Keys, Communicating with the 5 Generations in the Workplace* is the book to read. Employers & employees alike should read this book to become more knowledgeable & understanding of the people you work for and work beside. I believe after reading this book, you will recognize why there can be disunity and mistrust among co-workers themselves and between co-workers and management. The authors guide us toward solutions to increasing understanding and ultimately productivity and harmony across the generations who are in our workplaces."

Joyce L. Kelley
jkelley@gvcaponline.com

"This book, *10 Answer Keys, Communicating with the 5 Generations in the Workplace* is very enlightening about five generations: Traditionalist, Boomers, GenX, GenY, and GenZ. It conveys information about how to understand, manage, communicate and build meaningful relationships between these generations in the workplace. It defines each generation in areas such as communication, work ethic, time management, conflict resolutions, management, leadership, technology, buying styles, marketing, advertising, and values and visions. Mary and Meredith made this book entertaining, interesting and easy to follow. They definitely inspire me to look at each generation in a positive, enriching and unique way, and that each generation contributes to the workplace and the world. I believe everyone can appreciate and be enlightened after reading this book. In today's changing environment, this is a book that every organization and employee should have on hand."

Cecilia Clark
Quality Safety & Mission Assurance

Table of Contents

Table of Contents
(Cont.)

Why I Wrote This Book?

Mary:

In my work I encounter generational issues which often sit at the core of problems in the workplace. When we factor in gender diversity, cultural and heritage differences, along with personality dimensions, organizational charts, and salaries, the waters can get quite murky. It is just easier to expect people to function in what works for us. That is simply not so.

I have presented this topic as a workshop, and it draws people out into sharing their issues, experiences, and concerns. This brings about awareness, and awareness is the beginning of change!

I wrote this book to open up a dialogue between the generations. Stop condemning our differences and begin to respect them as a way to improve and grow as people as well as to provide a pathway to grow an organization. In my own experiences, adversity and diversity are places where I have gained amazing growth and new understanding. It may be hard, sometimes even downright painful, but in the end, if I approach this with the "okay God what are you trying to teach me here" approach, I grow.

I could have written volumes about this topic, but I wanted to give a concise yet powerful tool for my friends in business to use on a daily basis to improve their lives and offer the opportunity to improve their relationships with their employees and customers as well.

These tools can be used in personal lives too. Please transfer what you learn to your other relationships around you. The dynamics of those other relationships can be quite complex when you add dimensions of generations to the mix.

Meredith and I can facilitate the working relationships of the different generations within the workplace as a program. If you identify this as an issue that needs attention, please contact us for help.

It was Dr. Emerson Eggerichs who wrote the book *Love and Respect* that coined the phrase "**NOT WRONG, just DIFFERENT**." Applying this to my life has reaped generous rewards, so much so that it has become my mantra.

Cheers,

Mary

Meredith:

The world is changing. Growing up in this new world is amazing. I remember watching Star Trek years ago and seeing the incredible gadgets that they had, and now today it seems we all have them. Well we can't do the "beam me up Scottie" yet but who knows, the way the world is going, that could be on the horizon.

So why write a book on the various generations? I think many people are simply confused how to handle all the changes. I personally am a Boomer and came kicking and screaming into the technology field. Today I text my children because that is the only way I ever can communicate with them and have them respond. I have to Facebook my daughter-in-law and my extended family if I want to keep up on what is happening. My husband on the other hand prefers the phone when communicating although he will email.

I am still old school when it comes to my clients as I would prefer to call them and send them cards and letters (not emails or e-birthday cards) on special occasions.

In some of my speaking engagements, I have asked questions how individuals feel about how they would address the different generations. I find that there are mainly two camps. The one camp would treat the different generations as they would want themselves to be treated. The other camp would try to find a common ground that created a connection to the other generations. What I am trying to accomplish, with the help of Mary Erlain, my co-author, is to help find that common ground. There is nothing wrong with the first camp, but I think that in some cases they are missing out on helping many individuals that do not match their style.

So if you are serious about reaching the masses, and your business is not just a niche generation market, then this book may be of great value to your growth potential.

If we learn to speak the language of the people we want to help, it will be easier for them to like us and trust us.

Every generation has their own language. I know when I traveled in foreign countries, every attempt that I made to learn their language made my visits more enjoyable and endeared me to the hearts of the people I met.

Isn't that something we want in our business - that people like us and trust us? What better way than for us to speak their language? I know that's a goal of mine, and I hope for you also.

Every generation has a very specific wavelength, and individuals who have goods and services to market need to be aware of this.

With a Grateful Heart,

Meredith

Generational Language/Terms

We want to offer a few website links for you. As our generations have developed, so has our unique language. We will do our best to define unique terms for our readers, but if you need additional clarification, please check out these resources:

- www.internetslang.com
- www.anythings.org/slang/
- www.urbandictionary.com
- nws.Merriam-Webster.com/opendictionary/

Chapter Format

As with all our books, there will be a series of highlighted points at the end of each of our 10 Answer Key chapters called Answer Key Points. In this book, we have also included Application and Discussion Points along with Stories and Suggestions from each of us. Ideally, this will provide our readers actionable ways to use this book to go beyond the new knowledge gained, and to take it to the next level.

Survey Information

When we decided to write this book, we created a survey to see what the different generations felt about certain issues.

At the beginning of each key, you will see the survey question that relates to that key, and you will see the responses by the various generations for each of the questions.

We sent out over 500 surveys and received 122 back. In some case we had write-in responses to our questions and could not include those in our results. The results you see in our survey were based on the answer choices that were chosen by our participants.

We are grateful to everyone who took the time to answer our survey. We acknowledge our survey participants by name at the end of the book in our Contributors section.

Since this is a work in progress, we would love your feedback. At the end of the book is a copy of the entire survey. Feel free to take the survey either online at www.the5generations.com/survey/ or email Meredith at **Meredith@MeredithBromfield.com**. We will then update our results when we update this book.

Introduction

The 5 Generations Defined

Quotes:

What really distinguishes this generation in all countries from earlier generations... is its determination to act, its joy in action, the assurance of being able to change things by one's own efforts. ~ _Hannah Arendt_

The generations of men run on in the tide of time, but leave their destined lineaments permanent forever and ever. ~ _William Blake_

There is a mysterious cycle in human events. To some generations much is given. Of other generations much is expected. This generation of Americans has a rendezvous with destiny. ~ _Franklin D. Roosevelt_

There is a great generational divide that exists in our culture which began around 2011. This causes confusion, conflict, productivity challenges, customer issues, leadership and management gaps, overall tension in the workplace, and loss in revenue and profitability. How can we manage these gaps, and even more importantly, use them to our advantage?

Read on...

Our first goal is to clearly define each generation. Understanding the generations from a black and white viewpoint will then help us more clearly understand the grey zones. There is no one-size-fits-all, put someone in a box method here. There are Traditionalists (born prior to 1946) who are agile on a Smartphone and Gen Y's (1977-1990) who prefer to use a paper planner to track their calendar. Never assume.

As you read this, identify your own preferences. Perhaps create a page of notes for each employee, supervisor, manager, etc. to identify their preferences. As you do this, you will gain clarity as to how the generations work (or potentially are not working) in your company. This simple exercise can become the awareness piece necessary for change.

Here is a scenario to consider: the culture in your organization, when you consider your people, processes, and technology, aligns with Boomers (1946-1964). You hire a young Gen Y (1977-1990) or Gen Z (born after 1990) with the expectation that they should fit right in to how you do things, and then find them unhappy, non-productive, rebellious, critical, etc. This move may have the best intentions to try and get some younger people into the organization, but it sadly ends in turmoil and turnover. Typically, we blame the new hire for the problems and scapegoat them for all of "their issues." Let us ask you, "What is your part in it?" That question will get a myriad of responses ranging from a mystified look on one's face to frustrated finger pointing. As you read this book, we hope that you will gain much more clarity in understanding the answer to this question. We also hope that this book becomes your handbook for understanding the people around you with a heightened level of awareness and acceptance.

There is no one-size-fits-all management and leadership method other than clearly understanding what motivates your people. That sounds simple... understand what motivates your people; it is not so easy to do at times. The information we will provide you is just one piece in the puzzle to that understanding. It starts with you sincerely having a desire to personally lead yourself. This will be a brave move for some people. It will require a willingness to be brutally honest and open about your strengths as well as your weaknesses. Understanding generational preferences without judgment or condemnation will go a long way in developing yourself as a leader and manager of people.

We have heard about the four generations in the workplace. Why five? Our Gen Z's (born after 1990) are just beginning to get jobs as they enter adulthood. They are now in our workplace and deserve the attention to understand their qualities and preferences. With the challenging market conditions, as well as the entrepreneurial opportunities, some Gen Z's are starting their own businesses and becoming leaders in organizations where they are the bosses.

It is not uncommon to find Gen X'ers (1965-1976) and Gen Y's (1977-1990) in the position of ownership, leadership, and management of those older than themselves. This presents a myriad of issues that trigger responses. We will examine the parental projection issue more in depth when we discuss Leadership / Management and Conflict Resolution. Briefly explained, we bring our "stuff" from past experiences forward into the working relationship and begin to behave and act in that "role." These dynamics complicate matters that have nothing to do with our past, but yet become very real in the moment.

Going forward, we will define generational preferences within the bulleted topics below. We will also draw upon our research and our own experiences to provide scenarios and solutions to common issues that present themselves in our generational divide.

Each generation will be defined within these areas:

- Communication – Verbal & Nonverbal

- Work Ethic & Time Management

- Conflict Resolution

- Management & Leadership

- Communication In Media

- Technology

- Buying Styles

- Marketing & Advertising

- Values & Vision

- Passing the Torch

Between the time we are born to becoming adults, we will form powerful core values. These values will be influenced by our families, educators, peers, etc. Each generation has different values, ideas, ways of getting things done, and preferences in the way they communicate the above. Note the use of the word different. There are two methods and messages to those who are different from you, generationally speaking:

1. **DIFFERENT, therefore WRONG.**
2. **NOT WRONG, just DIFFERENT.**

Each choice has its own results.

Implications of lack of awareness –
DIFFERENT, therefore WRONG!

- High turnover rates

- Tangible costs (recruitment, hiring, training, and retention)

- Intangible costs (stress, culture, and morale)

- Grievances and complaints

- Negative perceptions of fairness and equality

Benefits of awareness –
NOT WRONG, just DIFFERENT!

- More effective communication

- Fewer misunderstandings and conflict

- Increased employee retention

- More effective motivational methods

- Realistic and appropriate expectations

- Increased productivity and teamwork

- More creative solutions to issues

You can rent their presence,

but you cannot buy their passion.

Let us define the generations. Please note that there are some slight differences that define the years of birth amongst various research materials. Again, there is no cookie cutter generation out there. We have adapted. The years that we use are guidelines in defining the generations. Please resist the temptation to take a black and white inside the box approach to the years. The point we are making is that between those years is a dash (-) and that dash represents the life and times in which that generation was influenced and defined.

Let's pause a moment and define values. Personal values evolve from circumstances with the external world and can change over time. They may be derived from those of particular groups or systems, such as culture, religion, and political party. We do allude to these when we define each generation. However, personal values are not universal; one's genes, family, nation and historical environment help determine one's personal values.

As we mentioned earlier, people also have their own ways to get things done, communicate and come up with ideas. These may be influenced by generations, and in addition, be determined from the level/type of education, personality dimensions and mental aptitudes, past experiences, family dynamics, etc.

As you review the next pages, again we encourage you to take notes. Perhaps purchase a separate journal to record your notes as you go through each of the Answer Keys. Use a highlighter to identify yourself in the generations that will be defined in the next pages. It may help you see how you possess qualities of other generations. It may also show you the beginning awareness of where you may have issues with other generations.

The consistent feedback we have received as we have presented this topic to groups has varied from eye opening and confirming to downright uncomfortable when participants are introduced to these concepts. If you experience these reactions, you are not alone. The key is what you do with this information.

The Five Generations

Through our research we have found that dates vary widely between the generations, especially Gen X'ers, (1965-1976), Gen Y's (1977-1990), and Gen Z's (born after 1990). There are no absolutes as it relates to these dates. Truly there is no one person who fits these values and traits perfectly. (Grab your highlighter!)

- **Traditionalists (born prior to 1946)**

    o **Also known as Radio Babies, Veterans, Seniors, or the Greatest Generation**

    o **Conservative**

- Fiscally prudent

- Loyal to their employers

- Practical

- Frugal

- Dedicated

- Respectful

- Heroes

  - President Franklin D. Roosevelt

  - Eleanor Roosevelt

  - Babe Ruth

  - Jackie Robinson

  - Joe DiMaggio

- Defining Events

  - Great Depression

  - World War II

  - Korean War

This generation brings a strong work ethic because they have grown up in the leanest of times and consider work a necessity as well as a privilege. They have earned their own way through their hard work. They are willing to put in long hours because of their loyalty. They are unique in that they often work for the same employer for their entire career.

They respect authority and don't tend to upset the apple cart. They will work well in teams of people who appreciate their effort and contribution.

They will be slow to adapt to the changes in the workplace. Technological advances can be both a mystery and a challenge for them. In their view, they may not see the need for technology as their conventional methods accomplished the tasks at hand quite well.

As for their personal development, a hands-on approach is preferable. Face-to-face interaction is necessary along with live lecture style formats. Online and other electronic formats will be a challenge for them to adapt to. Traditional business models with a top-down chain of command are what will feed their safety and security needs in the workplace.

As leaders/owners, the Traditionalists are fiscally conservative and are not very risk tolerant. They will possess more of a command-and-control style of leadership. Males in this generation are more than likely veterans and have acquired this style from their exposure to the military as well as their more paternalistic upbringing. They tend to set and obey the rules and have the same expectations of their employees. They have a desire to build a lasting contribution, and what they have contributed and accomplished to have a lasting impact.

Our Traditionalists have faced the toughest of times and have much to share with the generations. Providing them the opportunity to hand down this experience and knowledge in the work environment can have a lasting impact. The work environment has changed; there are nuggets of wisdom that our Traditionalists possess that can be valuable. Give them the respect they desire, appreciate their loyalty to their employers, and acknowledge their dedication to their work.

- **Boomers (1946-1964)**

  - ○ Ambitious

  - ○ Strong work ethic

  - ○ Loyal to careers and employers

  - ○ Optimistic

  - ○ Tendency to be workaholics

  - ○ Personal gratification

  - ○ Largest segment of workforce

- Heroes
    - Gandhi
    - Martin Luther King, Jr.
    - Mother Theresa
    - President John F. Kennedy
    - Jacqueline Kennedy
    - Senator Robert F. Kennedy
- Defining Events
    - Vietnam War
    - Woodstock
    - Women's Rights
    - Watergate
    - Civil Rights Movement
    - Birth of Television
    - Assassinations of:
        - John F. Kennedy
        - Robert F. Kennedy
        - Martin Luther King, Jr.

The term "Baby Boomer" is used to describe a temporary increase in the birth rate. After World War II and with the Great Depression having ended, the population exploded. Seventy-six million American children were born during this period. This also marked the growth of suburban living. A sharp contrast to city living, suburban homes were designed for growing families. Boomers control most of consumer spending.

Boomers grew up in a time of dramatic social change. It is possible to divide this generation **into two subsets**.

1. **Born prior to 1956**: Cuban Missile crisis, assassinations of John F. Kennedy, Robert F. Kennedy, and Martin Luther King, Jr., walk on the moon, Vietnam draft, anti-war protests, civil rights movements, riots, and Woodstock are events that epitomized the dramatic cultural changes of the 1960's. As a result this subset has a free-spirited, social cause oriented, experimental, and individualistic tendencies.

2. **Born 1956-1964:** Watergate, Nixon's resignation, the oil embargo, raging inflation, gas shortages, the Cold War, Jimmy Carter, Ronald Reagan, and Live Aid are the events that created this subset of Boomers to be less optimistic, have a tendency to distrust government, and possess a cynical viewpoint.

Dr. Benjamin Spock revolutionized child-rearing, urging parents toward a flexible discipline. The parent's role, he said, is to teach the child "the how and the why of acceptable behavior, but never at the expense of his sense of self-worth and optimism." Many Boomers grew up in households influenced by Dr. Spock's views.

This book's intention is not to focus on gender diversity, but in the Boomer generation, it needs to be said that the roles of women changed sharply. During WWII, women entered the workforce as the men left to serve in the military. After the war ended, women were urged to leave the workplace and embrace their roles as wives and mothers. Dissatisfaction in these roles contributed to the rebirth of the feminist movement in the 1960's.

Boomers have a tendency towards being workaholics. Hard work and sacrifice was the price to pay to be successful, and they wanted to make a difference. The way to have job security was to work harder than the person next to them. They enjoy teamwork and collaboration along with group decision making. They do not appreciate constant feedback or micromanagement.

As leaders/managers, they desire quality in their work as well as in others. They believe you must be prepared for the unexpected (which is why they carry two pens instead of one). They value and will want to keep to policies and procedures. Their ability to embrace change will be slow.

The aptitude to adapt to technology change can be diverse. We will see Boomers with the few flip phones that remain on the market. We will also see Boomers using Smartphones. The two subsets may distinguish some key differences in the Boomers adaptability to increasing use of technology in the workplace.

One area where Boomers have reinvented themselves is moving from being an employee to becoming an entrepreneur. Many factors have contributed to this trend. Most recently, the challenging market conditions, rising cost of employee benefits, etc. have created a serious issue of unemployment in the Boomer generation.

The Boomers have taken their retirement savings and severance packages to purchase franchises or start businesses as a way to survive.

Companies that do not attract or retain their Boomers will be missing out on one of the richest sources of labor that ever existed. This reality has come true as companies have focused on the cost of the Boomer generation in dollars rather than the value of the Boomers in loyalty, knowledge, experience and commitment.

Boomers have no intention to retire and see themselves as moving to a place where they work not because they have the financial need but have the desire to work as a way to achieve personal fulfillment. With recent market challenges that have led to a shift in Boomer employment statistics, it may not be financially possible to retire. Many of the Boomers are approaching retirement with significant amounts of debt. Much of that may be in credit cards as Boomers do have a tendency to spend beyond what they earn. In addition, they have had to face periods of long-term unemployment which has created a need to dip into retirement funds. Moreover, many issues that revolve around governmental programs such as Social Security, Medicare, healthcare, etc. have created a sense of unrest for the Boomers as they near retirement. I (Mary) will speak for myself, as a Boomer in subset #2, the future for the Boomers does seem a bit unclear as our time horizon in the workplace shrinks day by day.

- **Generation X'ers (1965-1976)**

  - 35% are non-white and 29% are legal immigrants

  - Most educated as compared to the preceding generations

  - Independent

  - Highest number of divorced parents

  - Dual-income families

- Self-sufficient (e.g., took care of chores and other responsibilities after school and before parents returned home from work)

- Realists

- Informal

- Result oriented

- Intolerant of bureaucracy

- Heroes
  - Not really influenced by any real heroes

- Defining Events
  - Collapse of Communism
  - Missing kids on milk cartons
  - Computers in classroom
  - Recession (1980s)
  - Persian Gulf War
  - Rodney King incident
  - The Challenger disaster

The term "Gen X" was popularized by Canadian author Douglas Coupland's 1991 novel, "Generation X: Tales for an Accelerated Culture," concerning young adults during the late 1980s and their lifestyles. Gen X'ers were born shortly before the introduction of digital technologies like Apple's or Microsoft's operating systems. They were interacting with computers from an early age which helped them have a greater understanding of its concepts.

Gen X'ers have been shaped by the experiences such as the emergence of music videos, open classrooms, inflation, single-parent and/or blended families, latchkey lifestyle, space shuttle explosion, widespread political corruption, inflation and recession, and post-Vietnam national malaise. They were at the start of the video game era, cable TV, Walkman's, and the internet.

As a culture, they were far more open to diversity in race, religion, ethnicity, gender identity, and sexual orientation.

With their exposure to the events that formed their culture, especially in the political landscape, Gen X'ers are far more capable of embracing change than their predecessors.

They were latchkey kids due to the demands for two-income families by choice or necessity and because of the rise in single parent families due to skyrocketing divorce rates. Open classrooms marked a change in the way they learned. As a result, these Gen X'ers were independent, self-sufficient, and resourceful from an early age. This perhaps defines their general disdain for authority and structured work hours and demands. The hands off management methodology is what they prefer.

Since they were exposed to technology from an early age, they can adapt quickly to new technology.

This generation saw their workaholic Boomer parents lose their jobs in the tough times of the 1980s. Gen X'ers are less committed to one employer as a result of watching their parents' commitment to employers end up in a layoff. They are eager to learn new skills and appreciate employers investing in their development. They do not lean towards the workaholic approach, but rather a work hard/play hard balance in their life.

- Generation Y's (1977-1990)

    o Also known as Millennials or Echo Boomers

    o Grew-up similar to Gen X'ers, but with a different parenting style (e.g., timeouts, no spankings, very protective parents)

    o Extremely conscious of global environment

    o Open minded and accepting of differences in race, gender, ethnicity, sexual orientation, etc.

    o Socially conscious

    o Concerned with personal safety

- Technology dependent
- Require work-life balance
- Heroes
  - Mark Zuckerberg
  - Steve Jobs
  - Bill Gates
  - Oprah Winfrey
- Defining Events
  - Oklahoma City Bombing
  - World Trade Center Bombing
  - Y2K
  - Columbine High School massacre
  - Afghanistan and Iraq Wars

Why are they called Echo Boomers....their parents are Boomers (1946-1964) predominantly. The Gen Y's have been pampered by their Boomer parents. They have been raised by a generation of "soccer moms."

The Gen Y's are the fastest growing generation in the workforce today. This generation does not expect to work with one employer for life. They have great career expectations and a desire to make a difference immediately. They want meaningful work and a solid learning curve. They can, with a click of a mouse, let thousands of their friends know about how their companies are doing.

They are family-centric in that the fast-track does not carry much appeal for them. They are willing to trade the high salaries and billable hours to focus on work/life balance. This can be viewed as narcissistic by the generations that have gone before them. Conflict and struggles can arise in the workplace when filled with generational diversity that includes the Gen Y's.

In addition, they crave attention and feedback. Again, this can be viewed as narcissistic, but let's look again at how they were raised. They were nurtured and cared for at an intensity level not seen in prior generations. We will get into the idea of Transference later in the book, but this is what is at play here with our Gen Y's and their managers/coworkers.

The jury is out on whether the term "tech savvy" applies or "tech dependent." Tech savvy would mean that they know how it works…tech dependent means that they know that they can't live without it.

This generation, which was raised in the computer age, sees the world as global, connected, and 24/7.

This generation has also been referred to as the "Boomerang Generation." They live longer with their parents than previous generations and return home when life circumstances arise. The recent economy and market challenges have created this dynamic to a degree as well. Rents in some areas have skyrocketed due to the demand for apartment housing caused by the foreclosure boom.

- Generation Z's (born after 1990)

    o Also known as iGeneration or Nextars

    o Instant gratification

    o Social

    o Open books (little kept private)

    o Communicate in short spurts

    o Crave constant and immediate feedback

- Digital natives
- Affected by 9/11, War on Terror, and Recession
- Hyper-sensitive to conditional changes
- Entrepreneurial
- Technology dependent
- Heroes
  - Steve Jobs
- Defining Events
  - Recession
  - Post 9/11 landscape
  - War on Terror
  - Boston Marathon Bombing
  - Global Warming climate changes
  - Social Media
  - BP Gulf oil spill

Our Gen Z's have been raised in the internet and digital age. Information has been a click away for this generation. As a result, the Gen Z's can naturally process information (and perhaps expect others to) at a faster rate. Like their predecessors, they are tech dependent. They have been exposed to mobile technology at an earlier age as the ability to own a phone has become more economical and common with the Gen Z's.

They are a generation of early adopters because of their ease in working with gadgets as well as the frequency of new gadgets, apps, etc. hitting the market. Look at the time span between black and white TV and color. Look at the gap in time between Apple product releases. The difference is huge!

They are also a socially conscious generation. They will be interested in how green their company is. They will be happy to take a stand and be proactive toward being environmentally conscious at work.

Our Gen Z's have a constant need for connectivity with their peers. They do this with ease through the internet. Smart Phones have made this possible. Social media and instant messaging are their communication channels of choice.

Their privacy standards are at an entirely different level than previous generations. Their lives become an open book on the social media sites. It is not uncommon for them to open their day with how they feel and close their day with a summary of the day's events to their friends. They have the ability to include images and videos to tell their story as well. This has created a bit of a dilemma in the workplace surrounding privacy issues.

This generation is very entrepreneurial in nature. The opportunities to open their own business have increased. It is not uncommon for this generation to run businesses that have employees besides themselves. With market challenges, a lack of job opportunities, and knowledge base being a click or swipe away, they, in some cases, have had no other choice but to start a business in order to earn a living.

The dynamics of business is evolving where significantly younger generations are in a place of ownership/leadership/management of older generation workers.

Answer Key Points

- Highlight key ideas.

- Create a separate journal.

- Answer the questions at the end of each chapter.

- Share your findings with others.

- Become the change you wish to see in your workplace.

Answer Key 1

Communication:
Verbal
&
Nonverbal

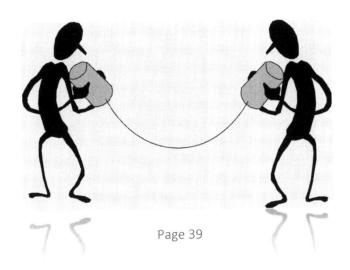

Quotes:

It is not so much the content of what one says as the way in which one says it. However important the thing you say, what's the good of it if not heard or, being heard, not felt.
~ Sylvia Ashton-Warner

Absence of communication between necessarily linked parties ensures eventual conflict. ~ Eric Parslow

There are three principles in a man's being and life, the principle of thought, the principle of speech, and the principle of action. The origin of all conflict between me and my fellow-men is that I do not say what I mean, and I don't do what I say.
~ Martin Buber

Meredith:

In our survey we asked the following question regarding individual's communication preferences.

What statement best describes your favorite type of communication?   Check only one.

☐ Email

☐ Face-to-face

☐ Letter

☐ Phone call

☐ Text

5 Generation Responses

	Trad.	Boomers	Gen X	Gen Y	Gen Z
Email	3	22	11	3	
Face to Face	4	42	15	7	1
Letter					
Phone		5	2	3	
Text		2	2	3	

What is it you want to say?

"Communication" is a critical component of dispensing information and letting others know what it is you want from them.

Methods of communication have components that literally transmit various signals to those listening that will either unite or divide them.

Most people have a tendency to run at the mouth rather than to have a clear concise mental picture of exactly the outcome they desire from their communication.

Communications was my major in college. Often my professors would explain that whenever there is communication happening between two people, that there are actually six messages being sent and received at any given time. No wonder people have a difficult time communicating. Add to the mix different generations and nonverbal cues, and is it any wonder that we ever understand each other.

Here are the six messages that occur whenever we are speaking to another person.

They are:

- What someone is saying?
- What someone is trying to say?
- What is actually being said?

- What someone thinks they are hearing?
- What someone is actually hearing?
- What someone is interpreting about what they are hearing being said?

Here is an example:

Person speaking:

What is being said: *I am sad.*

What someone is trying to say: *I am angry.*

What is actually being said: *I am very upset about this situation.*

Person hearing:

What was said: *I am sad.*

What someone is actually hearing being said:

You don't sound sad, you sound angry.

What someone is interpreting:

I am confused. You say you are sad, but you sound angry.

You can see that communication can become a rather complex venue. That is why oftentimes people get mixed messages, and there are numerous challenges.

The communication mentioned so far is on the verbal level, but it also includes nonverbal language as well. If we factor in texts and emails where the nonverbal is unavailable, we have now taken the concept of communication into outer limits.

Often, I hear people say it shouldn't be that complicated to just say what you mean and mean what you say, but that is very simplistic. Sadly enough communication doesn't often follow those rules. For example, if I say that I was just thinking about going to the mall and then pause to look sad, someone could interpret that I really didn't want to go to the mall. The fact is I may have thought of something that I needed to do before I went to the mall, or perhaps I remembered something I needed to pick up at the mall. My pause can be interpreted in a number of ways, and unless you ask for clarification or I mention why I paused, we could be on two different wavelengths before I finish one sentence.

One would think that talking on any level should be very simple, yet unless the listener is in tune to the speaker on many levels, there are many ways that errors in understanding can happen.

The key to communication, both on the verbal and nonverbal levels, is to make them match. When someone says they are interested but has a bored expression on their face, they are sending two different messages. The hearer might dismiss the words and rely on the body language to interpret what is being said. Truthfully, I have found that your body language is a much more effective determinant to what is being said, more so than the words or even the tone of the words. I think the emphasis on body language is well over 60% versus 30% for the tone of the voice and just 10% for the words themselves. Knowing that body language is definitely the major player in any kind of communication, what impact does this have on emails and texts that are being sent? I feel that one of the reasons that there seems to be more complications today than in the past is because a major component of communication, body language, is missing. This leaves the listener trying to figure out what someone is actually saying. So how can you help someone to better understand what you are saying? If we are working with face-to-face communication, there are a few things that we can work on and they are:

Making sure your tone and body language match your words. The best place to accomplish this is in front of a mirror. Look at yourself when you speak.

Answer the following questions when you are in front of a mirror:

Are you maintaining eye contact?

What is your posture? Are you positioning toward or away from your listener?

Are you standing in a space that feels comfortable to both of you? Everyone has a comfortable space surrounding them that allows for conversation; if you get closer than they are comfortable with, they will react and not listen to what you are saying. Watch their facial expressions. If they start looking uncomfortable, try backing up a bit to give them more space. If you invade their space and don't realize it, they will stop listening to you, and nothing you say will get to them.

What is the expression on your face as you are speaking?

Take cues from them as to their receptiveness to what you are saying. If you notice any movements that are different, take a breath and see if you just said something that they may have misinterpreted or maybe they did not like. Question them to see if you can get them to tell you what they think you just said. It may be that what you said and what they thought you said are totally two different things. Getting feedback from someone you are talking to is the best way to gauge if what you are saying is what is being heard.

Pausing during the communication process to gain feedback can save a lot of challenges and can insure that what is being said and what is being heard are in sync.

Are you making affirmative body gestures to show agreement to what is being said (Nodding, smiling, etc.)?

Are you listening to their responses? Are they reflecting what you just said? If not, are you taking time to clarify?

As you can see, communication is not just two people talking. It involves a whole lot more, and the quicker someone can master the various components of communication, the more they will be understood and trusted.

It is very difficult for someone to trust someone when they really don't understand what they are saying. When the words and the body language do not match, this is a death knell to any form of communication. Oftentimes, individuals who are communicating fail to recognize what someone is actually hearing; if that is not acknowledged, there is no true communication.

You can have the best dialogue, but unless the other person hears exactly what you are truly saying, and it is what you are actually saying, there will be no benefits as a result of your conversation.

Brief recap:

- Your words and tone must match your body language.

- You need to ask your listener what exactly they hear you saying and what they think you are trying to say.

- Until all parties involved in this conversation are on the same page, you are not communicating; you are just spouting words, and frankly you can save your breath because whatever you thought was going to happen just isn't.

Let's talk about the following generations and how they communicate verbally and nonverbally. This is crucial because each generation has a language of their own. If you are involved in any form of business where you are trying to get them to make a decision about some product or program, it is imperative that you understand the language they are speaking. When someone speaks their language, they feel more comfortable, and as a result have a tendency to trust what you are actually saying. Have you ever been to a foreign country and were so grateful when you finally found someone who spoke your language? In communication there is no difference. There is joy and a feeling of camaraderie as soon as they find someone who can speak their language.

Communication is a very broad topic and one that encompasses many styles. In every group that we will discuss, you will find some crossovers in the styles of communication. What we will do here is define the major components that are unique to each generation.

So let's explore the world of communication for the five generations.

Traditionalists (born prior to 1946)

Verbal:

Traditionalists are usually reserved in nature regarding personal issues. These individuals do not like to share personal information especially to anyone they don't know very well.

They have a wealth of information, but in most cases are reticent about sharing details about their family or their personal lives. These were the generation of people that never talked about what happened behind closed doors in their homes. They were not the kind of people who shared their feelings – everything was very personal.

They were very opinionated but in most cases would rather keep quiet than share what they were thinking. They were not confronters when controversial subjects came up except in the arena of religion and politics where they had some very firm beliefs and had very little tolerance for any opposing views. Until you really know them, do not expect them to open up, and recognize that in certain areas, they may never share.

On the other hand they, Traditionalists can be very direct if the topic covers areas that they have very strong opinions on. They are not afraid to argue a point or offend someone if they feel the other party is wrong or violates some sacred issues to them.

Nonverbal:

They have an entire vocabulary in their nonverbal expressions. This group was not raised in the verbal arena so their body language makes up for it.

Here are just a few of the cues that everyone needs to be made aware of:

- The crossed arms indicating I don't care what you say; I am not buying it.

- The rolled eyes indicating you actually want me to believe what you are saying.

- The raised eyebrow indicating doubt about what it is you are saying and wondering if you know what you are talking about.

- The half-smile indicating that I think I am beginning to see your point on this issue.

- The stare indicating do you really think you can change my mind about this.

- The walking away when they have had enough of whatever is going on. They have no qualms about offending you if you crossed the line in some way.

Boomers (1946-1964)

Verbal:

Boomers are the open and expressive generation when it comes to their verbal skills. They were given permission to tell it like it is, and they do. They are not intimidated with authority and have a general distrust of those selling products and services. They are the generation that voiced their anger over the Vietnam War and racial segregation.

These same verbal skills came with them when they entered the work force, and they fought for things they felt were injustices. They do not take things at face value and are not afraid to question and even challenge how things are done.

They are active in their beliefs and demand to be heard. When dealing with sales and advertising, they want the "good life" and everything that comes with it. They are swayed by ads and the desire to keep up with "the Jones" and the desire to flaunt their wealth. They are open and vocal about their desire to have it all. There is very little game-playing with this group as they will speak their mind and dispense with the guessing game of what am I afraid to tell you.

Nonverbal:

Boomers nonverbal skills are not as defined because they choose to speak their feelings rather than hide behind nonverbal cues. If they don't like something, they tell it rather than roll their eyes or cross their arms. If angered or upset, they would rather confront than retreat. They will leave an area when bored or upset rather than sit through a presentation with their arms crossed.

If someone says something that they feel is wrong or against what they feel is true, they will confront them.

They would prefer you to be honest and straight with them. Making them look for visual cues in your body language can hinder your communication with them.

They understand the various cues and will call someone on it if they appear bored or angry or emotionally unavailable based on their body language.

Mary:

Generation X'ers (1965-1976)

Verbal:

Gen X'ers are direct and want direct communication. They have had sufficient exposure to technology and prefer to use it to streamline their work efforts. Limiting the number of in-person meetings is preferable to the Gen X'ers. They desire to have a voice and often have a wealth of information to share. This generation often is squelched by the larger and more prominent Boomers. Look for those nonverbal cues of dissatisfaction.

Nonverbal:

Pushing Gen X'ers along with micromanagement will create an unhappy situation. They will be an open book in nonverbal ways when unhappy. They dislike the having meetings about meetings approach to business. Look for the subtle and not so subtle signs of disengagement such as aggression, daydreaming, rationalization, and repression. Understanding the reasoning behind certain actions – why people act as they do – can help you deal effectively with people when they seem completely irrational to you. All behavior is designed to satisfy some need, and even unproductive behavior in the workplace usually arises from some unmet, internal personal need.

Generation Y's (1977-1990)

Verbal:

Seek their input as they are on the cutting edge especially when it comes to anything technology related. This generation started the online social media wave. Think about how you can utilize them to bring your company into the 21st Century regarding online communication and marketing. Don't discount their youth in business or even think about communicating that to them in any way. They are confident, well-networked, and achievement oriented. They are job hoppers. Hone these traits to your advantage using communication skills familiar to them, and you can have a motivated Gen Y on your team.

Nonverbal:

Because so much of their communication is done using technology, they may be more unfamiliar to body language than the previous generations. Much of their communication is done using some type of media. They may not be aware of the cues that most would respond to. What they do respond well to and desire is lots of praise. The best way to develop the Gen Y in the workplace is to tell them often that they are on the right track and doing a great job. This must be done with a tone of mentor/coach, not parent. Remember, this is the Boomerang generation where the helicopter parents are there to take them in and support them in tough times.

Generation Z's (born after 1990)

Verbal:

Recently, I read an article that declared this the Facebook generation. Email is so yesterday. As I think about it, sending something to my son in an email is like sending something out into the abyss hoping for a quick response. Not gonna' happen! So how do we reach these people?

It does come down to doing what they do, painful as that sounds to many Boomers and beyond. Organizations need to embrace the idea of texting. Ironically, it may be the best way to get to people who owe you money since the overwhelming majority of texts are read in a matter of minutes vs. emails that may be read in a matter of days. Why not? Imagine how this may help your collections and sales departments?

Communicating to the Gen Z's (and Gen Y's too) has a different look to it. Just as in an email, where a different protocol is necessary to be effective, communicating to this generation needs to be in short and direct sound bites. Do not expect perfect grammar or spelling. Sad but true, it is not a priority to them. Instant gratification is necessary, so respond to them in a reasonable period of time...to them that measurement is minutes.

In organizations that wish to embrace this generation in the workplace, they will have much work to do to adapt their processes to accommodate the Gen Y's and Gen Z's. Remember, it is not the all-or-nothing approach that will be productive in any situation. The Gen Y's and Gen Z's will need coaching and mentoring to read emails and attend in-person meetings. It is in the compromise where communication can thrive.

Nonverbal:

Like their predecessors, Gen Z's are not completely aware of the nonverbal cues. If you detect a sense of urgency and impatience in them, you are usually spot on. Their lives have been filled with instant gratification in everything they do. They are simply wired that way. Resist the temptation to demean this in any way with your own nonverbal communication. Taking a leadership and mentoring role would be the most beneficial approach to provide guidance to facilitating a level of change or awareness.

The real takeaway in all of this is that each generation is different than the previous one. There may be stark or subtle differences that you observe. The reality is that the Traditionalists shrink in number each day...they still have much to offer if we just learn ways to approach them and give them opportunities to pass on the wisdom and experience they possess and learn to translate it into the current business workplace. Our Boomers are the largest of the generations in the workplace, but that doesn't mean they need to dominate as to how things are to be done. If Boomers are smart, they need to pass on their knowledge, mentor the generations after them and begin to Pass the Torch. Our Gen X'ers are a small but mighty group. They can be the bridge between the Boomers, Gen Y's, and Gen Z's. They have enough of the exposure to each generation and can be powerful leaders/managers. Our Gen Y's and Gen Z's are our future. The face of business will change whether we like it or not. We can hold tight to our outdated processes in communication and miss the opportunities that await us in the not too distant future. The heart of all of this is to embrace the idea to develop our communication skills and be aware of how these impact the people around us.

Mary's & Meredith's

Stories & Suggestions

Mary:

Most recently, I was presenting the 5 Generations workshop at a prominent Fortune 500 company in Illinois. I had one participant in the audience who was a Boomer. She was confused at how to "deal" with her younger (I would anticipate either a Gen Y or Gen Z) intern. Her body language conveyed a more maternal position, even in explaining this situation to me. The tone she used sounded "Mom-like" in its nature. The words she used clearly stated an "I'm right and she's wrong" position. The issue was around their differences in ways of communicating using technology. The intern preferred social media and texting, and the Boomer preferred face-to-face and email or use of the phone. I let her finish her story, taking stock of all of the verbal and nonverbal clues, and positioned myself to help her with the issue. I used active listening skills to clarify and validate what she said. I asked her a series of questions starting with whether she had children the same age as the intern. Using someone familiar to her seemed the avenue to help this lady move to a place of **NOT WRONG, just DIFFERENT**. I asked if she had raised her children offering technology as a way to learn as well as a source of entertainment; she had. I asked her if her school system offered technology as an approach to learning, and was she in support of this; she was. I asked her if she offered the latest technology to her children at appropriate times in their lives (i.e. cell phones etc.), and she had. Since the intern had been exposed to the same methods for her entire life, how reasonable was it to assume that she could adapt so easily to methods unfamiliar to her? The lady's eyes brightened as I spoke. Both parties were equally frustrated with each other and because of communication differences were clashing at each opportunity that presented itself. This small amount of coaching, along with the contents of the workshop (all found in the chapters of this book), set the stage to transforming a relationship from where the generations clashed to that of building a bridge between two people who truly cared about each other and wanted to find a way to communicate.

Meredith:

I am currently conducting a "Wisdom and Wealth Master Mind Group" in the area where I live, and there are different generations represented. In one of our sessions, I had a woman whose dilemma was how to effectively promote her business when a face-to-face meeting was not possible. The decision makers whom she needed to reach were predominantly Boomers and Traditionalists, and both of these groups rarely make decisions without meeting the other person face-to-face. Her business hours precluded her the time off to meet with these people. As we investigated various options, we came up with these possible alternative actions that she might want to explore.

- Hire someone who would represent her in a face-to-face meeting.

- Create a video where she profiled her business and spoke to the decision makers about the benefits of her organization.

- Combination - the person she hired would leave the video with the decision makers and conduct a face-to-face introduction.

As you can see, even though there may be challenges, there are always ways that one can come up with to make sure that each person's style of communication is honored.

Application:

- Make a list of people you work with.

- Categorize them into the various generations.

  - By age
  - By preferences (review Introduction)
    - Highlight similarities
    - Highlight differences

Discussion:

- Which group do you feel most comfortable communicating with?

  _____

  _____

  ○ Why?

  _____

  _____

- What group do you have the greatest challenges in communicating with?

  _____

  _____

  ○ Why?

  _____

  _____

- Recall someone you have worked with in the past or currently work with who demonstrates empathy in communication.

- Why do you believe they are good communicators?

  _____

  _____

- What qualities do you possess that they have?

  _____

  _____

- What qualities do they have that you need to work on going forward?

  _____

  _____

- Recall someone you know who is a great listener.

  _____

  _____

  o Why?

  _____

  _____

- What proactive steps can you take to better communicate with other generations?

  _____

  _____

- What resources do you need to improve your communication?

  - Coach
  - Classes
  - Books
  - Other: _____

- What resources do you need to provide your organization with to improve communication?

  - Workshops
  - Coaches
  - Courses/programs
  - Other:_____

Answer Key Points

- Communication is simple; it just isn't easy.

- Your words and tone must match your body language.

- Constant feedback is essential to good communication.

- Communicate effectively...you have one mouth and two ears – use them in that proportion!

- Improvement in communication does not happen by accident. It takes effort on your part.

Answer Key 2

Work Ethic &
Time Management

Quotes:

One thing you can't recycle is wasted time. ~ _Anonymous_

Time is the most precious element of human existence. The successful person knows how to put energy into time and how to draw success from time. ~ _Denis Waitley_

I suspect that American workers have come to lack a work ethic. They do not live by the sweat of their brow. ~ _Kiichi Miyazawa_

I am definitely going to take a course on time management... just as soon as I can work it into my schedule. ~ _Louis E. Boone_

Meredith:

In our survey we asked the following two questions regarding time management and work ethic.

What statement best describes your time management?   Check only one.

☐ Always late
☐ Fashionably late most of the time
☐ Late occasionally
☐ Never late

5 Generation Responses

	Trad.	Boomers	Gen X	Gen Y	Gen Z
Always late		1			
Fashionably late		3	3	1	
Late Occasionally	2	31	14	11	
Never late	5	33	13	4	1

What statement best describes your work ethic? Check only one.

☐ Cluttered but know where everything is
☐ Organized
☐ Cluttered but my secretary knows where everything is
☐ Job must be done
☐ Job must be done right

5 Generation Responses

	Trad.	Boomers	Gen X	Gen Y	Gen Z
Cluttered – knows where everything is	2	22	7	1	
Organized	3	24	9	3	1
Cluttered – secretary knows where					
Job must be done		4	1		
Job be done right	1	23	11	10	

As you would imagine, different generations responded differently to each of these questions. Before I get into what each generation typical answers, let's look at the two components: time management and work ethic.

Time management is very near and dear to my heart because I value every moment and understand that at any given time, there are basically three things that I can do with my time. I can waste it, spend it or invest it.

How can I waste time? I think for many people this is something that is done with regularity simply because the value of time is not intrinsic to their lives. Time seems to always be there, and many feel that there is an abundance of unlimited time. This is especially true the younger you are. Only as you age do you realize that there is finiteness to your time.

So how are we wasting our time? This varies from individual to individual, but whenever you are doing something or nothing with no purpose or intent, you are wasting your time. I know I was guilty of that on more than one occasion. In fact if I were put on hold when waiting for a call to connect, I would mouth those words "what a waste of my time." Rather than using that time to either spend it on something creative or invest it for future results, I allowed my circumstances to dictate my usage of time. I know personally I have spent hours on video games with the intent purpose of wasting time. This often happened when I was kept waiting to do something that I felt was important. Traditionalists' value their time the most and always have, maybe because they did not often have the luxury of excess time on their hands.

Spending one's time is what actually takes up most of our time. We do this by eating, sleeping, reading, working and a sundry of other activities that consume our days. Most of this time spent is part of our normal routines and habits.

Our best choice when it comes to our time is actually when we invest it for a future cause that benefits us or others. This is done deliberately and with conscious intention. This is mastery of time at its finest, and few understand and grasp the magnitude of this concept.

When it comes to time management among the different generations, this concept covers the spectrum from reverence to an attitude of indifference.

How the different generations view other generation's use of time is also very telling. One example comes to mind regarding the use of multi-tasking. The younger generations have mastered this, while the older generations, Boomers and Traditionalists, have often viewed multi-tasking as inefficient because of the lack of focused attention to the task at hand.

This brings up the second aspect, and that is work ethic. Work ethic and time management are often seen as kissing cousins since one generation perceives another generation's work ethic by their use of time management.

Talk about a time bomb in so many arenas when the various generations have to work together. As I mentioned in the aforementioned paragraph, the art of multi-tasking is a given to one generation whereas another generation may frown on it and make judgments regarding the quality of work achieved as a result. This is often an area of contention because to one generation the end result is the goal, but to another generation the process is viewed as the goal. This has often resulted in division and lack of cooperation when projects were needed to be completed. As Mary indicated earlier in this book, we are working on encouraging all generations to accept the concept **NOT WRONG, just DIFFERENT**.

Work ethic and time management are two areas where there seems to be very significant gaps among the various generations.

Traditionalists (born prior to 1946)

Traditionalists by their very nature have a very strong work ethic. To them work is up there with religion. Their value as an individual is very strongly tied into their work. They are proud of their work and who they are. Not working is tantamount to failure. Most of them have worked for the same company all their lives. They may have hated the job, but it brought a paycheck and they were satisfied. They were not looking to better themselves outside of the company they worked for. The thought of switching companies was unheard of, unless they were laid off or fired. They believed in the concept of hard work and would even go in when they were sick. I remember my mom walking 5 miles to work because there was a bus strike, and she couldn't miss a day of work. She lasted at Nabisco for 33 years. Taking a day off was unheard of.

Time management among the Traditionalists was a matter of honor and duty. To be on time was what an honest and honorable individual did; being late was like robbing someone, and it would be considered a very flagrant flaw.

Boomers (1946-1964)

Boomers also have a strong work ethic, but not to the degree of a Traditionalist. If they felt that the job was not meeting their needs, it was not unusual for them to start looking for something better. Usually they would not quit a job until they had something better. That would be foolish as far as they were concerned. They believed in hard work and doing a good job but not at the expense of their family or their health. They thought nothing about needing days off or using up all their sick and vacation days. It was a job, but if something better came along, they were gone, hopefully giving at least their two week notice. They realized that if one job did not provide the opportunities that they sought, then another job would. Bettering themselves was a core value that would ultimately get them better jobs with increased income and benefits.

Being a responsible group, time management was important, but if they were late occasionally they did not view it as a failure on their part but rather a situational event. They were cognizant of time and the role it played, but it did not govern who they were as individuals or their job performance. Their mantra was quality time versus quantity time. If they could do the job well in half the time, they did not feel it was necessary to do filler for the remaining time.

Mary:

Generation X'ers (1965-1976)

The Gen X'ers entered our workplace with a different work style than the previous generations. They place a premium on family time, and have a different attitude about work. **NOT WRONG, just DIFFERENT**.

Gen X'ers dislike rigid work requirements. They value a level of freedom to establish their working hours. As long as their production quotas are met, it is best to offer some flexibility. Rigidity will foster resentments and affect their performance and productivity. Flexibility will motivate this generation. Gen X'ers respond to mentoring. They appreciate regular feedback on their performance. Don't be surprised if they feel like they are "sandwiched" in your organization, especially if you have a generationally diverse organization. They have an entrepreneurial spirit which can benefit an organization if leadership is willing to tap into it. Don't forget the family life; create those events that incorporate family members. All of these small things can go a long way in encouraging a Gen X'er to perform at their peak.

To the Gen X'ers, limiting meetings to a minimum is a way to manage time. They do appreciate technology as a tool to manage time as they were the first generation who had technology incorporated to streamline their learning process.

Generation Y's (1977-1990)

I have read in multiple sources that the workplace will not even resemble what we see now when we move into the second quarter of this century. The reason why? Our Gen X'ers, Gen Y's and Gen Z's simply do not function like the Boomers and Traditionalists. We deem this later generation work ethic as a problem...are we taking the **DIFFERENT, therefore WRONG**, approach, rather than the **NOT WRONG, just DIFFERENT**, approach? Maybe there is a good chance we are.

Gen Y's are smart, tech-savvy, creative, and achievement-oriented. Because of their exposure to technology and social media, they are excellent multi-taskers. They prefer using technology to communicate such as email and text messaging. Face-to-face meetings are foreign to them... "don't waste my time making me come to your office." They do appreciate investment in education and development to learn how to streamline work. Web-based media is another way to help the Gen Y's save time.

Telecommuting is an attractive alternative to the Gen Y's. They are quite productive if given a familiar means for them to produce. They do love to stay connected if given the technology to do so.

If a Gen Y is to remain creative, motivated, and achievement-oriented, the culture in the organization must feed this. Work for them must be meaningful. How can you do this? They crave feedback on their performance as well as on how their work contributes to the organizational success. I hear your groans... "why must I have to do this?" Don't forget that they were raised (and continue to be raised in many circumstances) by the helicopter parents (who may be folks just like you). They have been conditioned this way. Yes, I know you are not their mother or father. I am not asking you to take on a parental role. I am asking you to be a leader of the talent in your organization that you are responsible for. You can either fight them and lose their talent and contribution potential, or for the overall success of the organization, you can find the areas where you can feed into their style. **The choice again is the results of DIFFERENT, therefore WRONG, or NOT WRONG, just DIFFERENT.**

Technology must be in place to manage time. They also want the ability to BLEND work into the rest of their lives. This is the crux of the problem for the Boomers and Traditionalists. This is a foreign language to them – blending work with life. Clear quotas, goals, and mentoring (not micro-management) will create a place for our Gen Y's to thrive. Don't know what that means Boomers and older? Invest in developing your own skills in order to develop your successors in business.

Generation Z's (born after 1990)

Gen Z's are the digital generation. They are wired for fast delivery of content. They have had and require a need for continuous feedback. This comes from their parents for sure, but check out most video games....constant feedback as well. They are multi-taskers and like the ability to have random access to information. Again, because of their exposure to gaming, social media, etc., they love to explore using their own pathways. It can be difficult for the previous generations to appreciate just how these employees are wired. They will appear impulsive in their decision making because long decision processes can be foreign and seemingly unnecessary to them.

They do not tend to be team players but are more self-directed. Investing in team dynamics enhancement would be helpful.

As with any generation, clear and defined results need to be communicated. Again, their performance and value to the organization needs to be shared with them more often than once per year in their review.

They want to be the leaders, and may indeed surpass the Gen Y's in this role. One of the critical differences between Gen Y's and Gen Z's is communication. They also communicate using video. If the Gen Z's want to learn something, they will find a video on YouTube, hence the explosion of the use of video in marketing as well as education and training.

From a time management perspective, the shear speed with which the Gen Z's process can be of value to an organization. The leadership has to be prepared to harness this talent and skill and to nurture the Gen Z's performance. They are like aliens in a workplace that is still operating in the Boomer mentality. Time, money, and resources need to be invested in the Gen Z's as they are the ones we will be passing the torch to in our near future. Give them the space, recognition, and direction to operate, and the results can be stupendous.

Mary's & Meredith's

Stories & Suggestions

Mary:

Through the work that I do with companies, my mantra has always been *"Focus on results, rather than process."* I was raised in an environment where the only way to get things done was my mother's way, and that even came down to which direction a table should be dusted in – apparently if dusted clockwise, the dust simply stuck to the table. When Larry Bird coached the Indiana Pacers years ago, he had to stop drawing himself into the plays when they were in clutch situations. He was in a suit and dress shoes, not shorts and his Converse Weapons.

It is difficult too for leaders to see the results in any other way than going through their process. In the world of time management and productivity, at the end of the day, it is about *results*. The simplest way to increase productivity is through goals management. The goal is the anticipated result. It is always best if the goals are determined by the owner of the goal. The goal can be massaged by you and the goal owner to modify it to fit into the organizational goals. If you just give the goals, quotas, etc. to the employees, there is no buy-in by them. They do not own any part of it besides the fact that they have the task of completing the goal or quota.

This will test your leadership and mentoring skills. There are plenty of tips throughout this book that will help guide you on what path you should take, depending on the employee. We have proven that it is not a one-size-fits-all pathway for you. If you invest the time on the front end to guide your people to productivity, the results (remember it is about the results) can not only be positive, but also sustainable. If you continue to struggle in this role, then invest in yourself... those skills can pay you over a lifetime.

As for time management, how one manages their time certainly has generational influences. I have been surprised to find Gen X'ers using paper planners, and Traditionalists agile on their iPhones. Time management and calendar management have much to do with previous exposure as well as to mental aptitudes and personality dimensions. One of the critical areas of concern is when any employee is keeping it all in their head. That is when intervention is necessary. *No Man Is An Island* is a great book, but also a great mantra for time management. Investing in skills development for these people is critical. Whether you realize it or not, keeping it all in your head does affect productivity. People must rely on those who "keep it in their head" to understand the next steps if they have not been written down anywhere. What happens if these people cannot be in the workplace? There are so many solutions out there, both paper and electronic, when it comes to managing time...none of these would be keeping it all in your brain.

To speak from personal experiences, I was one of those people who had the mental aptitudes and skills to keep everything in their head and rarely miss a beat. That was a lot of pressure. Through my own development, I am proud to say I don't need to do that anymore. I have, and continue to develop, my goals and time management skills. I plan my day the night before. I refine that plan in the morning and review the plan as the day progresses. I look at my week (and the next week) to create opportunities to be proactive on other projects. I "write" down everything I need to do and assign time to work on it. I lump up my tasks so that I am not shifting endlessly from an email to writing this book to a phone call. When asked what I am doing tomorrow at 2 PM, the answer is "I don't know, let me check my calendar on my phone." I live in the present and follow my plan. When life happens (and it always does), I pause and create a plan to deal with that issue.

The results are that I am not even the same person I was years ago. Those feelings come from many people from both my personal and professional life. How did I do this? I invested in skills development as well as, most importantly, my spiritual development and my relationship with God. **F.R.O.G.** – Forever Rely On God. Relying on myself just caused too much of a mess and stress in my life. Try it with the God of your understanding!

Meredith:

Since I started Wisdom and Wealth Master Mind Groups, my whole focus has been to help individuals to maximize their time and improve their work ethic. I found that in many cases that there were areas that seemed to sabotage their efforts from attaining the success they desired. One of the activities that I would have individuals do is to keep a chart for two weeks documenting where they spent their time and on what activities. This became very telling when they had to take the blocks of time they had dedicated to their work to see exactly what it was they were doing. It proved to be insightful when there were large blocks of time that were actually non-productive and would even be considered time wasters. These could have been activities that might better off have been delegated to someone else. Also consider that they might have only given the illusion of being productive when in reality they were of no value to the individual's goals for their success.

Application:

- Write down your preferences and strengths in work ethic and time management.

- Write down one thing that you appreciate about each of your associates' work ethic and time management.

- Write down one thing that you are having a difficult time accepting about each one of your associates when it comes to their work ethic and time management.

- If you work for a company, repeat the above as it relates to the time management systems your company uses.

- If you work for a company, repeat the above two bullets as it relates to work ethic and culture of the organization from your perspective.

Discussion:

- Which generation's work ethic and time management style has been the hardest for you to accept?

  _____

  _____

  o Why?

  _____

  _____

- How does this affect your own productivity?

  _____

  _____

  _____

- What steps have you taken to allow other styles in your work place?

  _____

  _____

  _____

- Are you willing to seek outside help to introduce other styles via training/development?

  _____

  _____

  _____

Answer Key Points

- Time management and work ethic are "Kissing Cousins."

- NOT WRONG, just DIFFERENT needs to be the mantra when multiple generations work on projects.

- If nothing changes, nothing changes.

- Nothing changes, if nothing changes.

- Historically, every generation believes they worked harder than the next generation after them. This can be a dangerous belief to hold onto.

- Work ethic means many different things to many different people.

Answer Key 3

Conflict Resolution

Quotes:

Whenever you're in conflict with someone, there is one factor that can make the difference between damaging your relationship and deepening it. That factor is attitude.
~ Timothy Bentley

The most intense conflicts, if overcome, leave behind a sense of security and calm that is not easily disturbed. It is just these intense conflicts and their conflagration which are needed to produce valuable and lasting results. ~ Carl Gustav Jung

Instead of suppressing conflicts, specific channels could be created to make this conflict explicit, and specific methods could be set up by which the conflict is resolved. ~ Albert Low

Mary:

In our survey we asked the following question regarding conflict resolution.

What statement best describes your first response when you are upset?   Check only one.

☐ Angry words face-to-face

☐ Blast them on Facebook

☐ Silent treatment/ignore them

☐ Text them your feelings

☐ Write them a letter

5 Generation Responses

	Trad.	Boomers	Gen X	Gen Y	Gen Z
Angry words – face to face	1	17	12	5	1
Blast Facebook					
Silent treatment	5	41	15	6	
Text feelings	1				2
Write letter		4		2	

For leaders and managers in the workplace, the first thing to consider would be to ask this question to yourself, is this conflict generational or is something else going on between individuals or within the team? One example of a generational situation would be that Traditionalists and Boomers do not like to be micro-managed, while Gen Y's and Gen Z's need specific instructions that are detail rich. Recognizing this can be crucial in finding a workable and sustainable resolution.

When you cannot apply basic generational principles to the situation, there may be other factors at play. Face it, some people are difficult to work with; they come in every conceivable variety. There might be issues related to their personal life that are being drawn into the work environment such as relationship discord, issues with children (or parents), siblings, friends, and other close relationships. You could also be dealing with health issues such as chronic illness, mental health issues, or perhaps issues related to addiction – substance abuse or other forms of addiction.

The reality is the situation will not get better if left unaddressed. It will usually get worse. One thing that will never work is complaining about the worker, either to the worker directly or worse yet to others.

Your responsibilities as a leader/manager include:

- Approaching the other person in a polite, problem-solving way to work things out.

- Avoiding actions (like gossip) that make the situation worse.

- A willingness to recognize that you have probably contributed to the problem.

- Listening to the other person rather than trying to convince or bully them.

- Seeking help from others in a dignified, open, and constructive way.

If you are involved directly in the conflict, these are some additional ways you can improve the situation:

- Start out by examining yourself.

- Don't take their behavior personally.

- Don't allow yourself to be sucked into the game, to fight back or try to beat them at their own game (adding fuel to the fire).

- Pick your battles.

- Don't try to appease them.

- Don't try to change them.

- Be very careful who you say things to and who happens to be around when you say them.

- Pause, breathe, think, and then speak.

- **Follow the Platinum Rule** (which should replace the Golden Rule): "Do unto others as they would wish unto themselves."

- Build a healthy relationship with a toxic coworker.

- Communicate well by listening with curiosity.

- Recognize their best assets and qualities and point them out.

- Focus on their strengths and positive attributes.

- Speak in "I" statements.

- Please keep in mind that you have both rights and responsibilities in these situations.

- Remain calm.

- Build a rapport.

- Understand the person's intentions.

- Get some perspective from others.

- Let the person know where you are coming from.

- Treat the person with respect.

- Focus on what can be acted upon.

- Ignore the irritating behavior.

- Escalate to a higher authority for resolution.

With this litany of ways to resolve conflict, let's look at the generations. Remember, each generation is holding to a set of core values. Appealing to these values can be a pathway to resolving conflict. The conflict, if generational, has perhaps stepped on or threatened a core value. This may have been done without a malicious intent, but rather out of one's own naiveté of generational differences.

Bring the parties together to encourage them to share their perceptions. We cannot change one's life experiences, but we can use those life experiences to our advantage. Look for common and complementary characteristics in the generations. I know this seems far-fetched. Traditionalists and Gen Y's have a similar tendency towards security and stability. Traditionalists and Boomers don't respond to change well, but they do crave training and development. Gen X'ers and Gen Y's place a lot of emphasis on work-life balance. Gen Y's and Gen Z's are most effective using technology. They also share a common focus on being socially responsible. When conflict arises, look to commonalities as a pathway to resolution.

Each generation has valuable lessons to share with the next generation. Create opportunities as a proactive measure to ward off conflict by using the generational diversity within your organization as a means to develop relationships. Traditionalists and Boomers have a wealth of knowledge and experience that younger workers need. Gen X'ers (1965-1976) are known for their fairness and mediation abilities. Gen Y's (1977-1990) are technology wizards. And Gen Z's (born after 1990) hold clues to future workplace, marketing, and business trends.

One example might be using the Gen X'ers to project manage a training program where the Traditionalists and or Boomers develop content for training and development. Involve the Gen Y's to advance the technology of the presentations, and encourage the Gen Z's to share their ideas on future trends as it relates to the content. Clearly defining roles, goals, and responsibilities around this project is most critical. Each member must understand their role and why they have been chosen, drawing attention once again to the core values.

No matter what the generation, when conflicts arise, as they will, using basic skills can be helpful. The reality is that the individuals want help, choices, and acknowledgment. The way they can attain those is if we listen, ask questions, reframe points of view in a positive way, and most of all...handle our emotions.

My greatest leave behind was given to me by a friend. In the face of any conflict, Q-TIP!

Quit

Taking

It

Personally

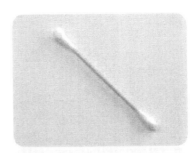

Go to your local market or dollar store and get yourself your very own box of Q-Tips. Keep one in your pocket, in your workstation, in the car, wherever you face your greatest challenges or temptations with conflict. Whether you are the leader/manager or the employee in the heat of the conflict, grab your Q-Tip in your pocket and hold on tight. Keep saying, Quit Taking It Personally! It will help you:

- Stay calm and remember: **it's not personal.**

- Be aware of the attitude you are projecting.

- Show willingness to resolve the problem or conflict.

- Find some truth in what the others are saying.

- Find out what they really want.

Once you have yourself centered in a place of objectivity that lacks emotionality, then:

- Put yourself in the other person's shoes.

- Paraphrase what they are saying.

- Acknowledge how they are feeling.

- Ask gentle, probing questions.

- Use "I" statements in your responses.

- Be proactive and positive in your approach.

- Stroke the individual (sincerely) – find something genuinely positive to say, even in the heat of battle (look for their core values).

- Never argue back.

- Use your ears more than your mouth.

- Show that you care.

- De-stress yourself as needed.

- Be patient.

- Keep in mind that angry people are not rational and are in a temporary state of mind.

- Avoid escalating the situation by becoming angry yourself.

- Let them relieve some tension by talking.

- Learn from your mistakes.

- Remember, it's **not a game of right or wrong**; it's a game of finding conflict resolution.

If you are the cause of the conflict, be the first one to:

- Seek to make things right.

- Apologize.

- Let the matter rest.

- Learn from your mistakes.

- Seek to appreciate their core values as a gift and pathway for your learning.

Meredith:

Conflict resolution is always such a hot topic. Mary did a wonderful job highlighting all the major points regarding each generation. My only and final comment is whenever you are in a position and there is conflict, the best thing I can suggest you say in the situation when it initially arises is "You could be right." This little phrase does not admit that you are wrong or that the other person is right. It allows you the opportunity to take time to analyze the situation and then to make decisions not based on the heat of the moment. So often people say trigger words that seem to suck people into conflict situations. Only later, when time has elapsed and someone has had the chance to really look at what has been happening in this given situation, can wise choices be made and clear-minded decisions prevail.

This little phrase has the power to stop the discussion in its tracks because it is no longer about a win-lose situation that is escalating, but rather about sending a message to the other person that says "You could be right, and right now I do not want to place myself in a position to argue with you nor do I want to." It is one of the most freeing phrases that you can have in your arsenal when dealing with anyone who, at that time, would like to create drama or conflict.

Mary's & Meredith's

Stories & Suggestions

Mary:

I would identify a few areas that are common in the area of conflict.

1. Lack of listening skills. People can be so busy thinking of what they want to say in response to the situation or individual that they miss the true message that is being delivered. Some ways to combat poor listening skills are:

    a. You were given one mouth and two ears – use them in that proportion.

    b. Take notes – force yourself into writing bullet points of what the other individual is saying. Then use active listening to summarize before formulating a response.

2. Leave the assumptions and baggage at home. As we will discuss in further detail, we bring baggage from all areas of our lives into the situation; the co-

workers have no responsibility for your hurts and harms from your past. If necessary, get a coach, join a small group, and get some help if someone in your workplace is triggering your issues from the past. This isn't to say that a co-worker may have responsibility for the conflict in the present, but it is unfair to make them pay for what others have done to you. In the generations, this can be grandparents, parents, siblings, partners, ex-partners, kids, and grandkids. Leave your family and their issues at home. Work on your boundaries.

3. Leading with your heart. This is similar to the above bullet. In negative conflict we leave most, if not all, of our objectivity at the door and lead with our emotions. That just simply clogs up the message and reduces the chances of creating a positive and/or workable solution. Yes, conflict can be emotionally charged, but the more objective you become, the more the ability to hear is increased, and the greater the chances will be to create a resolution.

4. All or nothing thinking. Compromise is just a ten letter word in the dictionary. Looking for areas to agree upon in the initial stages of conflict will begin to build momentum for an outcome. Find the smallest details that you can agree upon. Dig deep if you have to. Categorize the areas that you

disagree on, and then create the time and space to discuss those. Concession is not always defeat if the goal is understanding, growth and relationship-team building. A LOSE in any scenario is a lose for everyone whether it be lose/lose or win/lose. Build the WIN/WIN by mediating the conflict.

5. Reluctance to use a mediator. There are professionals out there that mediate all sorts of conflict. You don't need to be getting a divorce or taking someone to court to use one of these skilled professionals. I have a dear friend who is a retired pastor who holds not only his divinity degree but also a conflict resolution degree as well. He is a master at being the mediator and conflict coach. I have used him in my business and personal life with tremendous results.

6. Just because you are older does not mean you need to be the leader in the conflict resolution efforts. Avoid taking the parental role – it often can get in the way of the results. Create a climate that does not paint differences in a negative way. Acknowledge them and then position yourself to use those differences to your advantage. Review the Introduction to this book to identify where you can use the strengths of the generations to your advantage and thereby gain a positive resolution and build the team dynamics as a result.

Meredith:

Conflicts will arise from time to time if you are working in any kind of environment where there is interaction on a regular basis. The fact that we are humans and flawed denotes the propensity for conflict. So if it is an inevitable part of interaction in our lives, what are we to do?

I would recommend you ask yourself the following questions when facing a conflict:

- How important is this issue that is causing this conflict?

- Can I just handle the conflict with a simple statement like: "You could be right" or are there deeper issues involved?

- Is there something that I can change or do to make this conflict situation better?

- If there is something that I can do to resolve this conflict, why have I not done it?

- Are there triggers from my past relationships that are causing me to project into this situation? For example: the boss asked me to do something that was said in such a way that it reminded me of my parent, and this triggered a negative feeling. This often happens when the person is from another generation, but it can also be in the same generation when the past relationship is that of a sibling.

- What are some steps that I can take to make this situation better?

- Do I need to seek outside help to resolve this?

- What will be the benefits of resolving this conflict?

- What am I hoping to gain by not resolving this conflict?

The more honest you are in answering these questions when a conflict arises will allow you to see what patterns you have allowed in your life that creates or attracts conflicts. I have found that in many cases conflicts are repeated in our lives over and over again until we find ways to resolve them. The players involved in conflicts may change. For example, the conflicts when we were younger may have been with parents or siblings, and as we age the same pattern now shows up with persons of authority and with co-workers. The only way to break a conflict pattern is to identify it and then deal with it because patterns don't go away. In fact, they actually only get worse.

So for a final comment, when dealing with conflict, the challenge is to figure out what is causing it, especially if it is a repeating pattern. Then decide to find a way to resolve it. Your future depends on you finding ways to masterfully handle conflicts with all generations. If you fail to do that, you will find yourself in constant conflict with certain generations. I have discovered that learning to deal with all conflict, no matter who is involved, is imperative for one's success.

Application:

- Write down what you do when conflict arises.

  ○ Emotionally
  ○ Objectively

- Write down which ones are the most effective.

- Write down the scenarios that seem to be a reoccurring theme where conflicts seem to occur.

  ○ People
  ○ Situations

- Write down where you may be contributing to these situations.

  ○ Co-mission – meaning your participation contributing to results.
  ○ Omission – where your conflict avoidance may contribute to results.

Discussion:

- Do you find that you are having more conflicts with certain generations?

  _____

  _____

  o Why?

  _____

  _____

- Do you find that certain situations have trigger points for different generations?

  _____

  _____

  o Why?

  _____

  _____

- What have you found has been the most effective way to handle conflict for each of the generations that you encounter on a regular basis?

_____

_____

_____

- What are you willing to do to affect change in these scenarios?

_____

_____

_____

Answer Key Points

- Q-TIP...Quit Taking It Personally!

- "You could be right."

- Discover patterns in your conflict.

- Discover trigger points.

- Be honest, what is your part in this?

- Be the change.

Answer Key 4

Management
&
Leadership

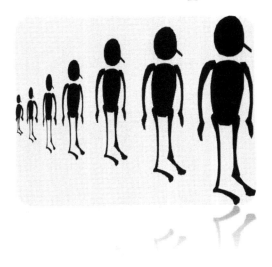

Quotes:

Effective leadership is putting first things first. Effective management is discipline, carrying it. ~Stephen Covey

Management is doing things right; leadership is doing the right things. ~ Peter Drucker

Management is about arranging and telling. Leadership is about nurturing and enhancing. ~ Thomas J. Peters

Management is efficiency in climbing the ladder of success; leadership determines whether the ladder is leaning against the right wall. ~ Stephen Covey

Mary:

In our survey we asked the following question regarding management and leadership styles:

What statement best describes your management and leadership style?   Check only one.

☐ I am the boss.

☐ I don't strive to lead.

☐ I follow my own lead no matter who is in charge.

☐ I follow whoever is in charge.

☐ I take charge when I realize there is a lack of leadership.

5 Generation Responses

	Trad.	Boomers	Gen X	Gen Y	Gen Z
I am the boss		6	7	4	1
Don't strive to lead	2	1	1		
Follow own lead		8	2		
Follow others	1	2	1		
Take charge	3	51	20	12	

First, let's define leadership and management. They are not the same thing. They are both required talents in an organization.

Management is defined by Merriam Webster as:

- to **handle or direct with a degree of skill**

- to exercise executive, administrative, and supervisory direction or *manage* a business

- to work upon or try to alter for a purpose

- to succeed in accomplishing

Leadership is defined by Merriam Webster as:

- to **guide on a way,** especially by going in advance

- to direct on a course or in a direction

- to **serve as a channel**

- to direct the operations, activity, or performance

- to go at the head of

- to guide someone or something along a way

Good leadership in any business is the true competitive advantage in the market. It is so often the last thing that business owners, especially small business owners, invest time, money, or resources into developing, both in themselves as well as in their people.

A quality of a great leader first requires them to possess exceptional talents in leading themselves in their day-to-day work. These skills revolve around productivity, accountability, strategy, and seeing and believing in the vision, mission, purpose, and values of the organization. In addition, great leaders need to attract followers. Sounds simple enough, but it is becoming increasingly difficult to accomplish this if we consider these numerous factors. Our market has had many challenges causing a shift in our workplace environments. It is now more difficult to attract the generations, and the diversity the generations bring, to follow one leader.

Meredith and I hear this said on a relatively frequent basis, "How do I motivate my people." Our answer is simple, "You can't." You can lead by example and avoid the "don't do as I do, do as I say" approach to management and leadership. You can understand the "WIIFM" (What's In It For Me) of your people. Understand their goals and the quality of life they desire outside of work. We are working for the life away from work, not to work. We can understand how our people need to be appreciated by security or recognition. Those who are security-focused need to know that they have a job to return to tomorrow, and that what they do brings value to the organization. These are not your risk takers...asking them to take a risk is a threat to them. Those who are recognition-focused are people who are willing to take the risk and desire the recognition. Incentives that can be used come in all shapes and sizes. My favorite is "great job" – not used nearly enough today in the workplace.

Transference

One article that was offered to me during this project was from the Harvard Business Review, September 2004, "Why People Follow the Leader: The Power of Transference." Reading this article (and I encourage my readers to get a copy online) was quite an eye opener for me. When we consider how transference works, it is not surprising how this can get in the way of generational working relationships.

Without getting off topic and turning this chapter into one about psychoanalysis, I will briefly speak to this subject. As I do, reflect on your own working relationships in the past, as well as the present.

- Those relationships that worked well and those that failed.

- Look at people who you see around you, but not directly related to you (either as a supervisor or a direct report) and observe where transference plays into the dynamics of their relationships.

- And finally, now look at the relationships closest to you and see where people may be practicing some level of transference with you as well as you with them.

A good idea would be to grab a journal and jot some notes down as you read, instead of keeping this all in your head.

Transference takes place when feelings for one person are applied or transferred to another. It's the boss who reminds you of someone in your early life, perhaps in your family, from your educational experiences, friends, etc. The dynamics of this can be alive and well in family businesses.

As one example, research indicates that when an employee identifies his/her boss in a parental way, the employee will move heaven and earth to please the boss. As long as this dynamic is supported by both parties, the employee will continue to work hard and produce. This dynamic does not always have to be the stereotype of the older boss and younger employee, although that would be considered the traditional and most common occurrence. This leader-follower relationship is also changing as the traditional family of two parents and children has developed into blended families, single parent homes, dual-working parents, and so on. The dynamics are not so simple. Now add the 5 generations into this mix, and the complexities multiply exponentially.

Another phenomenon can occur during organizational stress and transition. The proverbial apple carts of transference are upset. In times of organizational crisis, the leader is more focused on the crisis than the employee relationships. Needs are not met, and people react. These reactions can be displayed in many ways, mainly as a result of fears being triggered. Usually when fear is triggered, reactions surface at some level of fight or flight response.

During times of transition, especially in leadership, transference factors can play a huge part in stress. Trust issues and fears come into play, and coping skills are stressed. Often leaders are shocked at the responses of employees to change in the company. With this knowledge about transference, as well as we know, we are reacting from the values and conditioning from our generational influences. If we factor in current conditions outside of the work environment, it is not such a surprise at all.

When we have our older generations working **for** our younger generations, the transference can become quite confusing to all involved. Overcompensation for the age issues just adds to the problem.

A few key transference dynamics are:

Father: "Father knows best" – when there is one decision maker who presides over meetings. The message is very clear… "trust ME."

Mother: Maternal transferences generate greater expectations of empathy and tenderness from bosses than can realistically be met. Mothers were traditionally the ones who gave us unconditional love as well as the healthy "NO." This can create a lot of internal conflict.

Sibling: Simply put, competing to be the favorite of Mom or Dad. This can also cause employees to band together against a boss. Younger generations are very susceptible to this type of transference as they have had less exposure to traditional anarchic leadership. Peer networks are what they have depended upon.

So having said all of this you ask, "Now what do I do?" The first thing is to examine your own issues with transference, and how this may be playing out in your organization. This is probably not an exercise to work on alone as blind spots get in the way. Using a coach, consultant, counselor, etc. can help you gain an accurate insight. The key is to be honest. Understand where this is an issue for you as well as where you are promoting or enabling it to exist in others.

Be honest with yourself and your employees. Do not be something you are not. Keeping yourself on the pedestal will only encourage the issues to continue. Demanding perfection and displaying unrealistic expectations is not a healthy way to lead anyone. Provide the same environment for your employees. Be clear about written goals that contain action steps and accountability. You first! Create an environment that displaces the achievements from people to goals. This can ease the competition in sibling transference as well as the parental transference of the need to please an individual in some way.

If you realize your environment is filled with these issues, bringing in consultants and coaches can be quite helpful. Bring one in that has a belief in goal setting and has a clear plan to offer regarding the professional development needed to transition your organization into a healthier environment.

Management

Now with some understanding of transference, you should have some "aha" moments why things are the way they are. I defined management for you earlier. Management is based upon skills, tools, and results. The easiest way to manage the generations is to focus on their goals. With the following formula, any person in any generation can create ownership of their goals, taking into account the unique values and qualities they possess from their generational influences. The manager needs to be aware of these goals, not only the action steps and measuring results, but also the understanding of the WIIFM (What's In It For Me) of the employees' goals and managing the employee to reach those goals.

Here is the formula:

1. Goals need to be S.M.A.R.T. –

   - **Specific** – the details of what is to be accomplished in a clear and simple way.

   - **Measurable** – the goal must be quantifiable.

   - **Attainable** – it must be reachable considering ability, talent, and resources.

   - **Relevant** – does this goal match up to what the organization desires to accomplish?

   - **Timely** – there is a deadline to completing the goal.

2. Benefits & Losses – they define the WIIFM of the goal. This is not just organizationally focused, but focused as well on life outside of work. The more definition and detail to this section, the greater the chance of reaching the goal and perhaps exceeding it. This is where you allow the generations to own their values. The awareness of their benefits and losses creates ownership for the goal and the buy-

in to reaching the deadline. This is what you manage in addition to the results.

3. Obstacles & Solutions – yes, life happens. The first obstacle is always labeled "Me." Why? If it wasn't, the goal writer would have accomplished this goal already. There is some internal obstacle that stands in their way. This must be identified and solutions developed to address the weakness.

   Each obstacle, external and internal, to the organization is identified. With each obstacle, at least two solutions are developed. In the heat of obstacles and crises, we are driven by emotions and often make choices that were not ideal when we look back on them. Oftentimes these may have been choices that cost someone their job or did some other injury or harm to an employee. Guilt overruns us and gets in the way of our current productivity. If we consider crises scenarios before they happen, we can create objective plans that we just need to set into motion if and when the crises occur. If our first (and most optimal solution) does not work, we have at least one or two more as backup solutions.

4. Action steps with deadlines – ALL of the action steps. Let me explain through an example. If I wanted to work out three times a week, the action steps would look like this.

- First, do I belong to a gym? No.

- Do I know where all the gyms are in my area? No.

- Do I know what the cost is to join? No.

- Do I own workout gear? No.

- Do I need to see my doctor first for a medical clearance? Yes or No.

Okay, I have some work to do before I can work out at the gym three times a week.

- Action Step 1 – call my doctor and communicate my intentions, schedule an appointment as soon as available, and see the doctor to get clearance. (This may adjust the deadline because we are at the mercy of the doctor's office schedule).

- Action Step 2 – research local gyms and create a list by the end of the week.

- Action Step 3 – visit my 3 top picks by the end of next week.

- Action Step 4 – determine if I need to visit more gyms (and do visit them) or make a decision by the end of the following week.

- Action Step 5 – purchase workout gear over the weekend.

- Action Step 6 – join the gym, take the tour etc.

- Action Step 7 – begin my workout schedule.

Breakdown the steps in bits and pieces. Leave nothing to chance or assumption. Assign a realistic deadline to each step. Track the results of each step. Never erase adjusted deadlines…always keep track of the original goal's deadlines. This is added learning to help you refine your skills at building SMART goals in the future.

5. Accountability – who is the accountability buddy in this goal and who needs to know about it? The manager may be one partner, but sometimes being strategic about the generational influences may be a smarter move here. Consider the choice carefully.

6. Measurement & Tracking – this goal must be quantifiable. What methods are being used, and what schedule of reporting is needed to track results. We cannot wait until the deadline to determine we are off track. Too late. Tracking the goal is simply executing the "inspect what you expect" part of management.

7. Visualizations & Affirmations – develop clarity using the senses and create sustainable behavior

changes. Creating the end result in a picture or bringing the benefits of attaining the goal to life can be quite useful. Affirmations are a way to get control over that committee in our head that gets in the way of our results. It has been termed as head-trash, negative self-talk, etc. If we take control of some of our messaging and create simple positive phrases that lack the words "not, never, neither, can't, etc.," we can create a positive attitude of motivation. Instead of "I am fat" .... "I am a beautiful person who wears a size ___." Say it into the future. You may not be anywhere near a size ___; that's not the point. Speak the future into the present. Also, do not say "I am not fat; I am thin." The word "not" negates the entire phrase.

Another key leadership/management skill set is to have a sincere interest in understanding the strengths and talents as well as the areas in need of further development. There are many assessment tools available to provide this information. These assessments can also show where people are overcompensating for their perceived weaknesses. An example would be someone who is highly sensitive, in an attempt to cover his hypersensitivity to hurts and harms, may come across as edgy and sarcastic. Another example could be someone who comes across a bit too carefree and "que sera sera" about life but may actually be someone who has a deep need for security and has a strong fear base.

Additionally, exercises can be developed where employees understand each other's personality dimensions. Awareness can often melt away generational differences, and we can use our generational diversity to build the team.

If we identified a security focused Gen Y individual in an exercise (one that I conduct regularly), the Traditionalist in the group may serve as a great mentor. This can melt away the perception that this Gen Y doesn't care.

If the highly sensitive Boomer realizes that sensitivity can be a plus in business, the generations above and below might respond differently. They may see this person as crabby and unapproachable. Overcompensation abounds here, but with some awareness, understanding, and tools, this situation can be transformed.

As our Traditionalists exit the workforce completely and our Boomers begin to retire in larger numbers, the face of business will change dramatically. In the meantime, some things do need to change in companies sooner rather than later.

- Before implementing new workplace strategies, processes, and/or rules, consider where you are at, where you are going, and who the people are who will get you there. In the end, consider if this is the right avenue you should be taking. Gaining the input of your employees in this is critical if you wish to attain any degree of success.

- Ask for employee feedback on a regular basis and demonstrate your ability to take action upon their suggestions. Your ability to gain positive organizational results, as well as employee retention, is reliant upon these actions.

- Encourage communication...as proven in the Conflict Resolution chapter.

- Invest time, money, and resources in determining the engagement of your employees. These results will run parallel to the organizational performance, employee retention numbers, and the profitability of the organization.

- Encourage mentorship programs – not just the senior members to the junior members. We all have something valuable to learn from each other. Absolutely consider the generational preferences when delivering this information.

- Be aware of sudden changes in performance and results by an employee. Don't just dismiss it as a generational issue; dig deeper – show sincere interest - be a resource for additional training and support. If not handled directly by you, find the appropriate resources to address the problem.

Meredith:

Management and Leadership can be compared to going to a party where each generation is performing a different dance. While the Traditionalists are dancing the waltz, Gen Y is break dancing.

Traditionalists managed their people. There was a job to be done, and someone had to do it. There was someone who oversaw that the job got done and got done right. This group worked in environments where creative thoughts and ideas were not encouraged. There were a few companies that challenged their workers, but for the most part, it was a very top-down management style. As an employee in this environment, your goal was to get to those top tiers so that your voice could be heard, yet for many in this group, their main goal was to get a paycheck and enjoy the weekends. Work was just a job; it was not a way of fulfilling longing and ambition. It was a different world for these individuals, and the main concern was they had a job and that they took care of their families. Historically Traditionalists worked in a very male dominated atmosphere. Promotions were done by hard work, being responsible and having loyalty to the company. Bottom lines, innovative ideas, and competitiveness were not the setting of the Traditionalists group.

Boomers, on the other hand, were the first generation in which leadership was embraced and thinking by employees was encouraged. Bottom lines, competiveness, and new ideas were starting to rear its head. Women definitely started to make an appearance, desiring to change things in the workplace and to find their place in management. Management was soon to be seen moving over so that a new leadership style could emerge. No longer was the prevalent message "we do it this way or you're fired" communicated to employees, but rather "let me hear your ideas" was the new message. Suggestion boxes on how to make the workplace better were introduced, and great ideas were rewarded with bonuses and promotions. Management teams were encouraged to attend leadership classes and seminars. Business coaches were hired to analyze work situations to determine how individuals could work better as a team. The team concept of management and leadership appeared with more frequency as company owners realized that getting everyone involved made a company more productive. The next generation saw entire companies take these concepts to higher levels. Apple and Microsoft were some of the leading innovators of this concept of total employee involvement, and the results sparked a revolution around the world.

Even today the concept of leadership has continued to evolve. Companies are working harder than ever to get employees to have ownership in their company. Nordstrom is a fabulous example where employees are given the latitude to think and make decisions when dealing with customer concerns.

Right now we are in a flux as a nation as the age old concept "do what I say or you will lose your job" is making a slow comeback. The reason for this is a major shift in our economy. At one point someone who didn't like their job could quit, and usually within a relatively short period of time would find themselves newly employed by another company. Today with the shortage of jobs and the glut of employees on the market, some companies are reverting back to the old school of management in dealing with their employees. Leadership in the work force is no longer embraced, and in some cases not welcomed. People fear for their jobs and are willing to settle for less than perfect conditions because the prevailing attitude is "at least I have a job."

This, I feel, will change once again as the bulk of the population of Traditionalist and Boomers finally retire from the workforce over the next 10 to 15 years. The concept of working smarter, not harder, will take over leadership styles as the hard work ethic of the former generations will no longer permeate the work place. Innovative ideas will be rewarded, and leadership will take a very dramatic new look. Working long hours will no longer be the goal but will actually be viewed as a loss of productivity. Anyone who can find a way to do a job quicker and more efficiently will be rewarded.

Mary's & Meredith's

Stories & Suggestions

Mary:

In the past years, it has been the Traditionalists and Boomers in leading roles. In the next 10 years or so the tide will significantly shift. I (Mary) am 54 years old at the time, and in 10 years I will have an 18 year old grandson who will be, for all intents and purposes, in the workforce to some degree. There will still be 5 generations in the workplace, but I will take the place of our current Traditionalists. Wow! For me that puts things in perspective, like an icy bucket of cold water over my head. I look at how fast these first 8 years of my grandson's life have gone, and I realize the tipping point we are on right now and how quickly it approaches. We have two choices as leaders and managers. I will display these in pictures...

What I see are many companies run by Boomers predominantly taking the approach as displayed in the picture above. They may be sticking their heads in the sand as a result of being in denial about the issues or being in a state of overwhelm about the responsibilities in the day-to-day operations. The more you invest in your people, the greater the gain in the end when it comes time to finally sell your business. Those that take the ostrich approach will ultimately lose at some level whether it is talent/people, money, or potentially the entire company.

Another way the ostrich is prevailing would be fear. We covered fear-controlling styles in this chapter.

Being like the wise owl above, wide-eyed, aware, and proactive, can produce gains beyond your imagination. Investing in the reality of change now can position your organization to thrive when others will continue to struggle, be stressed, or fail. The workplace will look different in the future, there is no doubt, and the question will be, where will you be?

Awareness and change can be painful, that is a fact. Using the talent within the organization may oftentimes require humbling (defined as not proud or haughty) ourselves to learning from others that are our junior. That can be a Gen Y learning from a Gen Z. This can be the way to ease the pain of change. Re-read the definition of leadership and management at the beginning of the chapter, and ask yourself who can teach me something I need to know so that I can move this organization and my skill set forward?

Meredith:

My work background covered many different industries and jobs. My first job after high school was with Blue Cross as an enrollment clerk. At the time there were no female sales representatives or women in leadership. After college I entered the teaching field, and there I started to see women in positions of leadership as principals of schools. When I had my children, I entered the field of finances. I soon discovered that these doors were open to anyone who displayed the desire to achieve greatness. In this arena, your age, sex, or education were no longer the deciding factors for one's success. Everyone could write their own success story, determined by their work and performance. It was a great environment for someone who wanted the freedom to call their own shots. No one was there to dictate their work ethic or style. People chose to respond to those in leadership with either their loyalty to work as a team player, or by making their way to the top themselves and creating their own group. The beauty of this system is that they were in control of their destiny.

What I did observe in this group was the different generational responses to all this freedom. For some this was an opportunity to excel, and for others, they struggled with this new-found freedom.

Application:

- Create a list of leaders/managers in your organization.

- Identify the potential leaders / managers that you can develop as replacements in preparation for the time when your current employees will transition out of the company.

- Create a list of necessary skills for:

  o Managers – (results focused)

  o Leaders – (visionary, people focused)

Discussion:

- Where is transference playing a role in your relationships inside your organization?

  _____

  _____

- How are you contributing to this?

  ○ Positively

  _____

  _____

  ○ Negatively

  _____

  _____

- What are your organization's leadership strengths?

  _____

  _____

o Why?

_____

_____

• Where do generations play a role?

_____

_____

• What are your organization's leadership gaps?

_____

_____

o Why?

_____

_____

• Where do generations play a role?

_____

_____

- What are your organization's management strengths?

  _____

  _____

  o Why?

  _____

  _____

- Where do generations play a role?

  _____

  _____

- What are your organization's management gaps?

  _____

  _____

  o Why?

  _____

  _____

- Where do generations play a role?

  _____

  _____

Answer Key Points

- Things are changing again - fear is controlling management and leadership styles.

- Future leader's motto: Work smarter, not harder.

- Leaders create heroes; Managers want to be heroes.

- Great leaders were never born.

- It is mission critical to develop your next line of leadership and management in your company to remain competitive and have sustainable growth.

Answer Key 5

Communication

In Media

Quotes:

I can get a better grasp of what is going on in the world from one good Washington dinner party than from all the background information NBC piles on my desk. ~ <u>Barbara Walters</u>

Electric communication will never be a substitute for the face of someone who, with their soul, encourages another person to be brave and true. ~ <u>Charles Dickens</u>

New York Times, July 8, 1983
With so much information now online, it is exceptionally easy to simply dive in and drown. ~ <u>Alfred Glossbrenner</u>

Mary:

In our survey we asked the following question regarding their communication preferences in media.

What statement best describes how you get your information?   Check only one.

☐ I get my information from my friends.

☐ I get my information from the print media. (newspaper, books, articles)

☐ I get my information from the web.

☐ I get my information from TV, radio.

☐ I get my information through research from a multitude of sources.

5 Generation Responses

	Trad.	Boomers	Gen X	Gen Y	Gen Z
Friends					3
Print	1	3	2		
Web	1	6	2	2	
TV, Radio		4	1		
Research	2	21	13	4	1

Oh my! The area of multimedia has become quite complex. The first thought that comes to mind at the time of this writing is how a royal birth has been announced. Prince Charles was born in 1948. His birth was broadcast by radio along with the traditional announcement placed outside Buckingham Palace. Pictures in the newspapers were the first images we saw of the prince. Several decades later, Prince William's birth was announced over the news waves via radio and television. Our first images of this prince were the news footage of the proud parents walking out of the hospital carrying the new baby. We did not hang on to every contraction with updates. We were pretty much informed when the young prince was born and his weight was revealed. We now look at how we learned of the latest royal birth, Prince George. We knew when the parents arrived at the hospital and who accompanied them. We received progress reports of the labor. We tweeted, Facebooked, texted, and surfed the internet for updates using our phones, tablets, etc. We hung on every detail that we could get, and then the moment arrived when the young prince arrived. Even Prince George's mother intended to send the news out via Twitter, although I suspect her secretary actually typed the message. Communication in media has become the challenge that baffles us all in business, unless of course you are a consultant who does this for your business.

A cautionary note, this is one area that is definitely NOT one-size-fits-all. Our Traditionalists have become quite accustomed to the use of computers. I think about how many use Skype / Face Time, etc. to reach out to families far away, whether they are grandchildren who live out of town or soldiers who are overseas. Admittedly, I became agile in Skype when my son went to Oxford University for a year. Somehow having him that far away across the big pond seemed different to me, and I longed to see his face. When he was two hours away at school, the phone was fine. I cannot explain it, but I am grateful for this technology.

We can split media up into two classifications:

Physical media:

- Face-to-face meetings
- Group meetings
- Large meetings (conferences)
- Video conferences
- Word of mouth

Mechanical media:

- Email
- Letters/memos
- Newsletters
- Newspapers/magazines
- Texting
- Instant messaging
- Social media
- Blog / Vlog (video blog)
- Videos
- Misc.

The question is how do we overcome the barriers that our generational diversity has created?

A barrier is created when your chosen method of communication delivery simply does not get through. A few examples are:

- Calling a person and receiving voicemail
- Sending emails without a response
- Sending letters, memos and such without a response
- Presenting a 5 Generations live workshop and expecting the Gen Y's and Gen Z's to show up in large numbers

Yes, I have done several workshops and have had a handful of these folks show up. Why? Go back to the introduction; it is simply not their chosen method of information delivery. I wouldn't expect them to be there. I can get the information to them via webinar, social media, video, etc.

 Our Traditionalists do enjoy the newspapers, but at the same time are open to usage of technology as it will suit their personal needs. Show them the WIIFM (what's in it for me), and they will adapt. Seek their buy-in. Offer them the opportunity as well as the patience to learn.

The Boomers are more willing to invest in technology but still crave that personal contact. Face-to-face meetings are how they learn, build relationships, sell, etc. Personal growth is important, and they thrive in the face-  to-face workshops where conversations can be had in a "lively" fashion. Through the research we have done, we found an interesting fact: the fastest growing demographics in Facebook are women over 55.

 Gen X'ers do not appreciate the long meetings and can be happy without the face-to-face contact. They are all about efficiency. They are self-sufficient and anything that will help them increase that autonomy, they will buy into.

Our Gen Y's and Gen Z's are solely based in technology as a whole. It is no surprise why they struggle to be on board in

environments that converse in media by way of physical communications.

It can be a costly undertaking to shift a company to employ new forms of communication. I will not disagree. I ask you, do you know the cost of your communication barriers that exist right now? What is the cost in delays, distractions, errors, omissions, employee retention, customer retention, HR issues, conflict, and productivity (or the lack thereof)...the list goes on and on? It is possible to shed light on those numbers through the use of consultants, sales auditors, etc.

"On average, employees waste 1.44 hours each day on nonproductive activities." This is according to Joseph Carroll of Gallup News Service. This is NOT due to socializing with people or spending time on social media...this is PURELY the ability to get work done within the framework of an organization. Communication plays a large role in this.

How to deal with this debacle?

1. Create a committee of people to help you understand how they are successful in communication. Have them defend to you why their ways are successful for them. Listen to them! Have them share scenarios where they achieved success.

2. Reach for outside help such as a sales auditor. If you cannot find one, I can put you in touch with one. The 5-step process can diagnose the gaps with the KPI's (key performance indicators) to back up the results.

3. Look at your competition to understand what they are doing. I am in no way asking you to copy them exactly. The culture of your workforce is different. Nevertheless, data is always helpful to understand and to help make the educated choice.

4. Find the areas to build bridges between the generations. Taking the all or nothing approach is taking the **DIFFERENT, therefore WRONG**, approach. It will cost you dearly. Where can you invest time, money and resources to build these bridges, perhaps training and development of your older workforce as one example? Invest in coaching and team dynamics development for your team. Companies that invest in their people are historically valued higher than those that do not.

5. Start with the end in mind. What is your BHAG (Big Hairy Audacious Goal)? Where do you want to be 10, 20, 30 years from now? Back it up; while considering your workforce, what do you need to do in this communication area today that will become positive steps toward your goal?

6. Don't fire all of your Boomers and Traditionalists! Go back to the introduction of this book and review every area that highlights them in each Answer Key. They are critical puzzle pieces in your growth going forward. Use them to your advantage. Their experience can be valuable as you seek to build bridges and move your organization to a healthier place where all your generations can thrive.

7. Keep your customer focus as part of every conversation. Circle back to what drives your company, and you will find that it is your customers. Help your organization develop plans that use the communication media that drives effectiveness, efficiency, and profitability. The best way to do this is to incorporate a generationally rich group to help you in these efforts.

8. Invest in surveys, assessments, etc. to gain insight into the gaps in employee and customer engagement. Don't do the surveys or assessments without the willingness to invest the time and resources to take action on the results.

Meredith:

Communication in the media is a mixed bag of messages. We recently did a survey, and the most prevalent way that individuals wanted to communicate was face-to-face. That being said, the odds of reaching everyone in my market face-to-face are very daunting. So how do we get to our audience?

Traditionalists are old school; they love letters and things that they can see or feel. Ads that depict people they can relate to and trust are important to them. An ad on the web or on television touting the benefits of an item is not going to encourage them to run out and purchasing it. Trust issues are paramount when it comes to their level of commitment to any product or service. Ads that use actors who have a trust level will hold their interest far longer than simply touting the benefits of a product by some unknown individual. Actors who played roles of integrity in their careers hold higher esteem when a product is promoted. Traditionalists enjoy paging through ads and enjoy print pieces. This generation grew up around catalogs and buying things that they could connect with on a sensory level.

Boomers are split into two groups: those who relate better to the Traditionalists' type of communication and the younger Boomers who are more apt to go online and order items. Trust is still a very big issue to this group, and any communication that doesn't address this will fail to reach this audience. There are Boomers who have embraced communication via the internet and their phones, but the majority is not in that group. They still would prefer the face-to-face when it comes to any type of communication. If this is unavailable, then the phone would be their next choice, with the letter being the last alternative. This group is not going to respond to texts, as this is probably the least personal mode of communication. They have embraced some forms of social media such as Facebook, but that seems to be a place for sharing pictures of grandchildren and catching up on what is happening to relatives around the country. Some have braved LinkedIn for business communication, but basically have simply posted a site with the hope that it takes care of itself.

If this is your target market, then any opportunity to present yourself as an expert at a luncheon or meeting would be the best dollars spent to reach both the Traditionalists and the Boomers. Trust issues are paramount, and if they can bring a friend to the event who can later agree with them that you are worthy to be trusted, you will have reached a major milestone in your relationship with these people. Having former clients bring new people to a meeting or event takes what you have to say to a much higher level of trust. Also never underestimate the power of someone who has had a bad experience with you who might sabotage your efforts. Building solid bridges, even if it means losing money to keep a client happy, will have much greater and lasting effects on your efforts to communicate with these generations.

Mary's & Meredith's Stories & Suggestions

Mary:

I use my favorite question, "How do you prefer we stay in touch." I also state my preference when I want to schedule time together. I prefer email to schedule appointments. When people call me when I am in the car, I cannot access my calendar in my phone. When I am reaching out to get together with someone, I also offer either a face-to-face meeting or a phone call. I will also text people when I arrive at a coffee shop/restaurant for a meeting.

There are professionals in the market who are experts in the world of communication using media. When using these professionals, make sure you engage one who has a track record of success with their clients. There are those I have come across who are self-proclaimed experts but possess little in the way of education, experience, and all around expertise. Just because someone is an avid social media participant who posts updates regularly, does not deem them communications experts in media strategy.

Meredith:

Communication is all about relating to the other person. I find that when I am relating to an older person, I will either call them or, if necessary, write them. I find the written word speaks volumes to them. On the other hand, when I communicate with the younger generation (Gen X, Y, or Z), I inevitably will text them. As far as my Boomer friends, I usually will email them or Facebook them. In some cases a phone call or text might be appropriate.

As you can see, we now live in a world where there are many options with which to communicate. The most crucial consideration is to know who you are communicating with, and what method works for them. I love to text, but I realize that my husband will never respond to texts whereas my children only respond to texts. It would be foolish of me to try to change either of them to suit my needs.

Bottom line for the people you interact with is to find out how they want to correspond and then accommodate them. That will endear them to you and make them realize that you care. At the end of the day isn't that what we all want, for people to like us and trust us. Communicating in their media of choice is half the picture.

Application:

- Create a list of your clients and their demographics as it relates to the generations.

- Create a list of employees as well.

- Create a process chart to diagram the communications in your organization, both physically and mechanically.

- Create a communications committee with generational diversity.

- Identify your communications leaders who are Traditionalists and Boomers.

Discussion:

- What are your communication preferences?

  _____

  _____

  o Why?

  _____

  _____

- Where are you having challenges in communication as it relates to media?

  _____

  _____

  o Why?

  _____

  _____

- Are you willing to invest time, money, and resources to assist in improving your communications process and creating a plan that can allow for change over time?

  _____

  _____

  o   Why or why not?

  _____

  _____

- What is holding you back from using other forms of communication media?

  _____

  _____

  o   Why?

  _____

  _____

Answer Key Points

- **Face-to-face is still #1 when it comes to Traditionalists and Boomers.**

- **If nothing changes, nothing changes.**

- **Communication in Media is not a one-size-fits-all for the generations.**

- **What is the cost of your communication gaps currently?**

- **What is the cost of change?**

Answer Key 6

Technology

Quotes:

Technology is so much fun, but we can drown in our technology.
~ Daniel J. Boorstin

Technology: No Place for Wimps!
~ Scott Adams

Once a new technology rolls over you, if you're not part of the steamroller, you're part of the road.
~ Stewart Brand

Technology is dominated by two types of people: those who understand what they do not manage, and those who manage what they do not understand.
~ Source Unknown

Meredith:

In our survey we asked the following question regarding use of technology.

What statement best describes your feelings about technology?   Check only one.

☐   I am comfortable with technology.

☐   I came kicking and screaming into technology, but now I am ok.

☐   I love technology.

☐   I tolerate technology.

☐   I understand it most of the time.

5 Generation Responses

	Trad.	Boomers	Gen X	Gen Y	Gen Z
Comfortable	2	20	8	3	1
Kicking & Screaming		1			
Love	1	4	7	2	
Tolerate	1	5	1		
Understand most time		12	3	1	

Traditionalists (born prior to 1946)

I have found from my experience working with this group that they are somewhat comfortable with, and most of them tolerate, technology. As I look at the results of our survey, we did not have a large enough population to give us accurate readings. Whenever I make general statements, I always remember the bell curve in statistics, where 80% of the population is in the middle and 10% are on either end. So if you are in either of the 10% categories, please take these statements as generalities, not things written in cement. I know that there are people in this group who are extremely savvy with technology and love it more than life itself. Yet, at the same time, there are an equal number of individuals who don't even own a computer. The key whenever you are addressing these types of topics is to try to be general enough so that it will encompass the majority population of any group.

Traditionalists realize that technology is something that their kids and grandkids use, and if they want to stay in communication with them, they will need to be able to at least understand email. They do surf the internet, but it is mainly for the news and occasionally to look up something. They are not going to spend an inordinate amount of time online. They will not do their shopping there, nor are popup ads going to grab their attention. They find them annoying, and too many will usually cause them to get offline. As far as the other modes of technology, smartphones, texting, instant messaging are still not at a comfort level that they embrace. Most of the new gadgets have way too many bells and whistles to be a comfort. They are still of the mindset that if I want to talk to you, I just need to pick up a phone, and in doing so not have to deal with all these complicated things.

Boomers (1946-1964)

Boomers on the other hand have found out that they <u>have to</u> plug into technology on some level. This may be limited to just opening an account on Facebook or emailing their children and grandchildren. Business professionals though have learned that finding their way around a computer is not an option if they want success. They will attend classes on social media and learn other basics in order to survive in the technology age. Do they love it? Some do, and some have come kicking and screaming into the technology age but have adapted wonderfully. If they are in business, then having a relationship with technology is a given.

As far as the other mediums, iPhones, Notepads, texting, instant messaging, some have made the step up but not all. They may have embraced the new smartphones, but for the most part, they are only utilizing limited portions of it. The same goes for almost any technology. They will find the things that they enjoy or understand, and leave the rest. They will seek out help if they are having problems accessing a feature that is important to them. But for the rest, they just don't care. It is more work than it is worth, and trying to remember all the various programs taxes their brains. Boomers do not live in a world of technology of "more is better" but rather "keep it simple but give me value."

Mary:

Generation X'ers (1965-1976)

Technology for Gen X'ers is all about self-sufficiency. That is their view of technology. How can this make them faster, better, smarter, etc. Gen X'ers are not into wasting time, and face-to-face meetings are a waste of time to them. They will acquire any skill and tool necessary as a means to an end. For them it is not about entertainment, but rather efficiency and effectiveness.

Technology is woven into the fabric of all areas of their lives. The focus once again is to use it as a means to an end, whatever that end may be. Remember, the Gen X'ers are not like the Boomers. Work/Life balance is critical for them. They have watched the generations before them suffer the consequences of the workaholic mentality. Technology for them is a way to create that balance through saving time and needless travel/communications.

This generation does possess one characteristic that many others do not, and that is adaptability. They are comfortable with technology, call it technology aware, but are not necessarily savvy like the generations after them.

Generation Y's (1977-1990)

Gen Y's have used technology consistently from a very early age, starting with their little V-Tech toys and moving towards video games and such. They will immerse themselves into new technology whether it is work or entertainment. It is their path to knowledge, social interaction, shopping, education, and entertainment. It has been ingrained into their lives by their parents, teachers, friends, coaches, etc.

Why then are we complaining so loudly when Gen Y's are not adapting to technology-sparse or archaic workplaces? This is what we created (speaking as a parent of two Gen Y's). Let's go back to Answer Key 5 and address the topic of hiring. It may be quite useful to include questions regarding technology in your interviews to determine how wide the gap is between a particular Gen Y candidate and your company/beliefs. It can save your company time, money, and resources if you determine a proper match early on in the interview process. This is opposed to when you have invested in a candidate who is not a match for the position or is not adaptable to your current work environment.

I have heard on many occasions business owners saying we need to bring in younger blood. How are we going to "Pass the Torch?" My response is usually asking the hard question, "Are you positioning yourself to bring these people aboard and to retain them? What does your technology in your company look like? When was the last time you had an IT audit to determine where you stand in relation to your competition and the general market?"

It is simply not the case to find some qualified Gen X, Gen Y, or Gen Z and hire them. In the end, unless you have taken a serious look at your communications and technology and put thoughtful planning in place with actions to address the gaps, you will be doing an incredible disservice to every single person involved, including your existing employees.

Generation Z's (born after 1990)

Here are some general statistics that I found in several places:

- Gen Z's are engaging with technology within 5-30 minutes of waking.
- Average connection time – 5 hours per day (not counting work).
- About 50% remain "plugged in" during sporting events / religious events / work.
- Nearly all visit YouTube weekly, but at least 50% visit multiple times per day.
- They are active contributors to comments on websites/blogs.

- Why are they online? Three reasons: to stay connected in relationships, to be entertained, and to learn new things.
- At least 75% agree that technology helps them reach their goals.

To our Traditionalists and Boomers especially, it is like our Gen Z's are aliens from another planet. Watching a group of them out to dinner can be so confusing to other generations. They are not "listening" or "talking" to each other. Very little conversation is going on, oh but wait. They all have a phone in their hands, and they are thumb typing wildly. Technology is simply how our Gen Z's connect with each other.

Technology is how they connect with the world. In my youth, I had a pen pal in Peru, and the only way we connected was a few times a year in a letter. This was the only person I really knew who lived anywhere internationally. Technology and social media provide the ability for us to connect to almost anyone, almost anywhere. Gen Z's knowledge of news, trends, events, etc. is amazing. To others before them, this may have been a passive activity, but to them it is part of their daily needs.

Technology is where Gen Z's learn. YouTube is one source for videos; explore this website, and you can learn about anything, anytime, anywhere. There has been a shift in our marketing to include videography as a means to deliver knowledge and to market our companies. There is continued demand for this type of learning.

Recalling from previous Answer Keys, Gen Z's process at lightning speed. In order to sufficiently absorb this generation in the workforce, a company has to be able to embrace their styles, needs, and pace. This is not a job for the faint-hearted or for one who does not see investing in their employees as a means to success. Gen X'ers, Gen Y's, and Gen Z's are not as loyal as those generations before them. If they are not feeling that the company appreciates them, invests in them, respects their knowledge, insights, etc. they bring to the workplace, they will leave.

Gen Z's have a business acumen that is also quite high. This is due to their exposure and curiosity to businesses across the world. They possess the ability, confidence, and wherewithal to start their own business. The shift is happening as we speak. What kind of businesses do Gen Z's typically start – technology-based of course.

Mary's & Meredith's

Stories & Suggestions

Mary.

Meredith and I used technology to convey the 5 Generations on the cover of this book. We know there are many factors that influence the generational differences. World events, education, experience, and economy are among them. The one seemingly obvious dividing line is technology. We can look at the changing face of the workplace as a land of opportunity, as opposed to a problem. The ability to deploy new technology systems and resources needs to be a thoughtful process. It will have a significant impact on business performance. With planning wrapped around the deployment, you can increase the chances to improve productivity, increase levels of quality, shorten sales and delivery processes, improve customer service, and ultimately drive revenue and profitability.

One simple idea, what happens when you end a face-to-face group meeting? What do your people do? Do they all spring to their feet to check their phones for texts, emails, and voicemails? How are they communicating with each other? All of this is valuable data to help you make critical technology decisions.

Again, reviewing the Introduction chapter can help you begin to put a plan together. This may require some necessary changes and/or rebalancing of your workforce, whether the person is 20 or 65 years old.

The good news is that technologies are becoming increasingly user friendly which can allow those less familiar with technology to be on board themselves more easily. Regardless of age, it is always important to understand how employees are wired. There are those early and late adopters in all generations. It is mission-critical to understand how they learn, what their preferences are, and how quickly they move along the learning curve.

As we have mentioned already, one idea may be to include pointed questions about technology preferences in the interview process. It might be helpful for you to identify potential gaps. If your company is simply not ready to hire someone who is either agile or averse to technology, best you find out early.

Encourage dialog why people want to communicate in a way different than you or your company. This dialog may be quite helpful in understanding where you are behind in the market. There may be hidden opportunities for your company to gain ground in growth.

I would strongly invest in coaches/trainers for your people. Not just for those who are technology averse, but for everyone so that a good work flow and established work process can be agreed upon. Left to their own devices, employees may use technology in ways that are not optimal for your company.

If you wish to promote creativity within your work groups, use technology such as video conferencing. There are those in the workforce who are less willing to look people in the eye in a conference room and share their opinions, especially if they are different. Put them behind a computer screen in an environment where they are safe, and they begin to open up. The threat for them has been removed.

Technology also allows for the ability to monitor employees. I would encourage that this be done in a positive way. Don't see it as a means for Big Brother to drop a hammer when performance is less than optimal. Consider it as a way to incentivize and reward employees.

Encourage proper usage of technology in conflict situations. More on Conflict Resolution in Answer Key 3.

It is always best to ask someone, "How do you want me to stay in touch with you?" This provides an immediate level of confidence and can avoid lost relationships, time, deals, and employees, etc.

If communication issues continue to arise, it may be helpful to reach for resources in teaching effective communication techniques. Of course, the format of this training should always bridge the generations and be offered in a variety of means to meet the needs of the workforce as much as it possibly can.

Shifting our focus to the customer, technology, at the end of the day, is the largest determining factor of whether a business flourishes or fails. With the presence of 24/7 internet, it has become the expectation by customers to have 24 hour access.

It is far too easy for companies to post reviews about your company. It is also very easy for them to research your company using a variety of resources. Many review boards have sprung up with industry focus. Online companies flourish as referral sources which share customer reviews, one being Angie's list. Yelp contains real-time reviews. Social media is also a hotbed for information on not only your company but your people as well. The tangled web we weave continues to grow. And you say, "Not everything I read on the internet is true." Yes, you are correct. But it is the customers who will draw their own conclusions and make the final decisions.

I will repeat myself here because this is, in my opinion, the most critical question you can ask someone in communication. Ask your customers how they prefer that you stay in touch. "Write this down" somewhere. If you have CRM (Customer Relationship Management) system software, then create a field to include this information. Create reports to understand and track how technology over time is shifting this. Ask one additional customer service question as follow-up to create the data you need to stay abreast or ahead of your customers' needs: "Ms. Erlain, is 'xxx' your communication preference?" where 'xxx' might be a formal letter, email, voicemail, texting, etc.

Meredith:

Technology is the wave of the future, and every day it is advancing with new and better methods of reaching the masses.

What I have learned is there are four different types of individuals in our world when it comes to embracing the innovations. Here is an abbreviated look at each of these personalities and how they relate to technology.

First we have the structured individual who sees technology as a time saver and very useful. Their world is very structured (you can recognize them by the order they have in their offices and homes). Technology to them is a given as it helps them stay organized and allows them to control their world.

The next group is the techies, and they die and go to heaven every time a new gadget comes out on the market. They want it; they want to know how it works and every aspect of it. They love technology, and their world is dominated by the devices (you can recognize them by the number of gadgets that they surround themselves with, and they also have a tendency toward piles, although they know where everything is in those piles). My husband is a techie, and when we went to buy our first car, the first question he asked was "what are all the options available?" Needless to say we bought a car with every option.

The next group is your movers and shakers – action people. Their middle name is "just do it." They don't want to know how something works, just that it does. They like the latest gadgets of technology because it allows them to make more things happen in a shorter amount of time. The more a device can streamline their world so that they can make something happen, the happier they are with the device.

The final group is our relationship people. Technology for them is just a means to an end to help them stay in touch with people they care about. So if that means learning how to email or Skype, then they will. Their end result is "I want to stay in touch, and if you have something that will help me do that, then all the better." They will buy the iPad because they can store pictures of their children and grandchildren. Technology to this group is a means to an end, not an end-all.

The beauty of these four groups is they coexist and will be found in every generation. So if you can recognize them, it will help you to connect with them on a much deeper level.

Application:

- Make a list of the technologies you currently use in your workplace.

- What technologies is your competition using to gain an edge in their business?

- Create a survey for your employees to learn what technologies they use both professionally and personally.

- Where's the gap?

- Create a field in your CRM system (any company in sales should have one of these) for customer communication preferences.

Discussion:

- How much does your organization invest on a yearly/monthly basis on technology?

  _____

  _____

- Where is technology the source of issues in your business: conflict/productivity, customer retention, etc.?

  _____

  _____

  o Why?

  _____

  _____

- Can you identify the generation gaps in the usage of technology, or are the lines very grey?

  _____

  _____

  o   Why?

  _____

  _____

- Have you identified the REAL cost of not upgrading your technology?

  _____

  _____

Answer Key Points

- Technology has become more user friendly, allowing generations to embrace it more easily.

- Technology is not a one-size-fits-all for the generations.

- What is the cost of your technology gaps currently?

- What is the cost of change?

- Are you ready to bring a new generation into your workforce?

- "[Person's Name], how would you prefer we stay in touch with you?"

Answer Key 7

Buying Styles

Quotes:

The 1990s customer expects service to be characterized by fast and efficient computer-based systems. ~ Steve Cuthbert

The propensity to truck, barter and exchange one thing for another is common to all men, and to be found in no other race of animals. ~ Adam Smith

Thank God we're living in a country where the sky's the limit, the stores are open late, and you can shop in bed thanks to television. ~ Joan Rivers

Meredith:

In our survey we asked the following question regarding buying styles.

What statement best describes your buying styles? Check only one.

☐ I do my shopping online - Amazon, Online stores etc.

☐ I look for bartering or exchanges - Craigslist, eBay.

☐ I shop where I have no one bothering me.

☐ I would prefer face-to-face sales.

5 Generation Responses

	Trad.	Boomers	Gen X	Gen Y	Gen Z
Shop Online		14	4	2	
Craigslist EBay		2		1	1
Shop where no one bothers me		8	1	1	
Face to face	4	20	13	1	

Traditionalists (born prior to 1946)

Traditionalists are by and large a face-to-face group. They want to engage as many of their senses as possible when buying a product or service. They also want to gauge the sincerity and integrity of the person they are doing business with. Your meeting with them face-to-face speaks volumes to them. You are communicating to them that they are important, that you are willing to sacrifice your time to actually meet with them. If your message, both verbal and nonverbal, speaks of integrity and trust, chances are they will do business with you. If at any time they catch you in a lie or a fabrication, your integrity is shot, and you might as well move on. Once trust is breached, very little will gain back the confidence of this group. Claims on your product that are questionable or seem to stretch the truth will negate their trust in you, and the sale will not occur. If there are issues that are circulating about your product or service that are not favorable, bringing them out immediately will show that you are not hiding anything. If they hear something about your product and you failed to mention it, your integrity will be eroded.

Another significant issue is that the value of an item is more important than its cost. They place more worth on quality versus quantity. They desire an item that is designed to last a long time and to live up to its claims. Again, it all goes back to the integrity of the item sold and the integrity of the person selling it.

Boomers (1946-1964)

Boomers run in groups with the majority still wanting the face-to-face when it comes to sales. This is especially important when it comes to big ticket items or when engaging the various senses is crucial to coming to a decision. Also trust issues are important but not to the degree that the Traditionalist has. They are more apt to want to feel friendly to the person and feel that their concerns are being addressed in this purchase.

A recent trend shows a large group of Boomers are turning to the internet to shop. This has proven to have some very worthwhile benefits that this group has embraced. Here is a short list of why shopping online makes sense to them, and why the population is growing in this arena:

- Allows for comparison shopping

- Not being hassled by a sales person

- Convenience of shopping online

- Saving money on gas – as prices go up, looking for ways to save becomes more important

- Saving time looking for items

- Can shop 24 hours a day – no time constraints

- No need to get dressed to go shopping (you can shop in your pajamas)

- Ability to create a wish list

Boomers want bargains. They are the epitome of getting a bargain. They love coupons and want to feel that they got the best deal of the century. If they find out that someone bought the same item for less, that does not bode well with how they feel about you or your product. Companies and services that give them price matches and guarantees of a refund or a better deal if the item sells for less somewhere else, makes them very happy. Any time you can underpromise but overdeliver will result in loyalty to you.

Not making them happy when something goes wrong with the product or service will result in more bad press than you can imagine. They will let the world know that you messed up. I had an issue with a return 5 years ago where the store refused to give me an in-store credit because I didn't have receipts for gifts given at my daughter's shower. I was very upset and even talked to corporate about this issue, but they stood on a poor policy that made me go back to each person who had given a gift and ask them to hunt down a receipt. I told everyone about the incident, and I have never been back to that store.

Mary:

Generation X'ers (1965-1976)

Many of the Gen X'ers were raised during some difficult economic times. Their tastes are not "Boomer." Because they have many needs and greater financial restraints, they often shop at value-oriented retailers. They can be unsure of themselves and often need reassurance that their choices are sound. They buy with a focus on work/life balance. They like products that will make things more efficient and practical. Gen X'ers like flexibility and dislike long-term commitments. They are not as loyal as their predecessors. They demand trust to the point that if it is violated, they will likely leave. They desire a relationship to the point of being treated like family. They will offer the same to you as a business owner. However, they are not terribly loyal to brands or companies.

They typically have families and need to buy products and services for their homes and children. There are a significant number of them that are single parents. They want to hear about the features of a product, but at the same time, they need to understand why these features are important. They are cautious and sophisticated as buyers. They do their research prior to buying, as they are agile in technology. They must feel that you know your product and service, and that they are getting a fair deal with not a lot of rules, stipulations, or commitments.

Generation Y's (1977-1990)

Selling to the Gen Y's is successful when you appeal to their belief that they can make the future better. They can be selfish, living just for today, and spend impulsively. They need to know that your company's mission speaks to a higher purpose than just a profitable bottom line. They also look for companies that are an "instrument of change."

Because of their early exposure to technology, they do grasp concepts quickly. Gen Y's do have a desire to learn, so put yourself in the position of teacher/mentor instead of a traditional sales professional. Help them understand the experience of owning the product or service that your company offers.

They are very peer oriented in their purchasing. Peers are their guides in their buying. They are early adopters and are open to exploring new paths and options. Personal image is very important. Tattoos, body piercings, etc. are not uncommon for this generation.

With all this being said, it would be helpful for mentors to educate Gen Y's regarding their buying, helping them make choices that have a longer range focus that considers the impact to their decisions. By no means am I criticizing this generation or suggesting we intervene in what they do. It is rather an opportunity to educate in a kind and loving way without control.

Generation Z's (born after 1990)

Image for the Gen Z's is very important. They are independent shoppers. Their helicopter parents are also buying merchandise for them, usually high quality and label/brand oriented. Young celebrities have capitalized on this generation with their personal brands, such as Selena Gomez, Jonas Brothers, etc. Instant gratification is a driver for the Gen Y's.

Technology is a tool for their buying. They have not had a day go by in their lives where technology was not a part of it. They have the latest phones, tablets, iPods, etc. and know how to use them. Devices are frequently replaced with the latest release or upgrade.

Music, fashion, cosmetics, and video games are important in terms of peer acceptance and fitting in. Car manufactures have realized this and have shifted their marketing efforts accordingly, and this in turn has influenced parental spending.

This generation is heading for serious health issues because of their lack of exercise and the foods they ingest. It may be helpful to attract this generation to gym memberships that are sold to meet their needs and desires.

Mary's & Meredith's

Stories & Suggestions

Mary:

One-size-fits-all sales training can create issues in the selling process. Consider the traditional sales process...

Prospecting → Pre-Approach → Approach → Presentation → Handling Objections → Close → Deliver.

Now consider all of the information you have acquired about the generations. Can you see where the process can get murky? Just the prospecting step in itself can become so vague when you take communication and technology into consideration. It may be best to consider an operational audit of your entire business development process. This can help you understand your Strengths, Weaknesses, Opportunities, and Threats (SWOT) in all areas of your sales process as well as to help you establish a forward strategy based on those findings.

It is true that people have a desire to buy; they buy what they FEEL they need, but the generational differences do create some challenges that need to be addressed.

Meredith:

We all desire items and products in our lives, and develop buying styles that dominate our purchases. When I was a young girl, my mother would hand me an Alden's Catalog, and I would select everything I wanted. Boxes would arrive at my home, and I would have my own fashion show selecting what I wanted to keep and returning the rest. Today I still enjoy buying online.

Our childhood memories hold a lot of clues to our buying styles. The era in which we were raised in, along with the influences of the media, economic, global and entertainment worlds, all are factors in our lives. I think of those people who grew up during the depression and developed an aversion to banks, or the Boomers who lost most of their retirement savings in the 2008 crash and now fear the stock market.

History needs to be our teacher in understanding what events influence each generation's buying styles.

Application:

- Create a list of demographics of your customers.

- Create a report from your CRM on what your customers have purchased.

- Create your:

  o Steps of the Sell - how you sell

  o Steps of the Buy – how your customers buy

  o Gaps?

- Do a SWOT analysis.

Discussion:

- What business have you "left on the table" as it relates to the generations buying your products and services?

  _____

  _____

  o Why?

  _____

  _____

- What areas are your strengths when it comes to selling to:

  o Traditionalists?

  _____

  _____

o   Boomers?

_____

_____

o   Gen X?

_____

_____

o   Gen Y?

_____

_____

o   Gen Z?

_____

_____

- With what generations are you not achieving the level of success you desire?

_____

_____

o Why?

_____

_____

- Have you identified a gap(s) where your organization could improve its selling success?

_____

_____

- Are you willing to invest time, money, and resources to educate your sales force in generational specific selling?

_____

_____

- Do you have a plan for your organization that allows itself to re-align with new generations that will ultimately dominate the purchase of your sales and services?

_____

_____

Answer Key Points

- Underpromise and overdeliver.

- No matter what generation you are selling to, be educated, honest, and responsible.

- One-size-fits-all selling processes don't work anymore.

- In sales, seek to understand generational need and influences.

- Seek opportunities to be the mentor of generations that come after you.

Answer Key 8

Marketing
&
Advertising

Quotes:

The very first law in advertising is to avoid the concrete promise and cultivate the delightfully vague.
~ <u>Bill Cosby</u>

We grew up founding our dreams on the infinite promise of American advertising. I still believe that one can learn to play the piano by mail and that mud will give you a perfect complexion. ~ <u>Zelda Fitzgerald</u>

The most important service rendered by the press and the magazines is that of educating people to approach printed matter with distrust.
~ <u>Samuel Butler</u>

Meredith:

In our survey we asked the following question regarding their marketing and advertising preferences.

Which statement best describes how you want someone to sell you something?   Check only one.

☐   I hate advertising.

☐   I love to read ads in newspapers, magazines.

☐   I prefer face-to-face advertising.

☐   I tolerate ads on TV.

5 Generation Responses

	Trad.	Boomers	Gen X	Gen Y	Gen Z
Hate ads	1	7	2	1	
Love ads	1	8	8	1	
Face to face	2	13	5	3	
Tolerate ads		13	2	1	1

Marketing and Advertising

How to reach the people I want to use my products and services.

Traditionalists (born prior to 1946)

Traditionalists are old-fashion, down home type of people. They like things they can make contact with whenever it is feasible. They are need-based in their desires. If they need it and they can afford it, they will purchase it. They will look for bargains, but will not make that the decision maker. They will respond to ads that come across as being honest and sincere. They don't want a lot of hype and bogus claims, nor are they into silly or dumb ads. They feel they have worked hard for their money and want to make sure that there is value in what it is they are buying. Ads that are stupid, sexual, or make no sense do not appeal to this age group.

They are not adverse to print pieces but will not make a decision to buy from that alone, although it may pique their curiosity enough to look closer at the product or service.

Testimonies from people they admire and trust go a long way in helping them to take a further look at a product or service.

Boomers (1946-1964)

Boomer's take on marketing and advertising is pretty much that they are just tired of it all. They were the first group that really got hammered with advertising. They also were the first group that bought it all up. They made decisions based on the ads we saw and heard. They learned the jingles, and even today there are Boomers that can sing the commercials of yester years. I think at this time the Boomers are saturated. They realize that what is said does not make it so. They are jaded and tired of all the stuff flying at them from all avenues. They have come to a realization that 27 ads for items promoting weight loss will not actually help them to lose weight, but are in fact simply designed to sell products. They are fed up with the hype, the corny ads, and the sex sells ads, and would love to find products and see ads that actually address a concern or provides a solution. They are wiser and more wary when it comes to spending their money. They had lived above their means most of their lives while believing the ads, but now find themselves in a tougher situation. They too want value and to make their life better, but they are not going to jump on every bandwagon that is propagated because from experience they just know better. They want value, but they also want the best price available. They are not adverse to shopping around and even demanding that products and services live up to their expectation. They are the largest consumers on the planet, and they want respect regarding their time and money. They are tired of any marketing strategy or ad that overpromises and under delivers; this will be met with disdain and anger. They see this as a personal affront to their intelligence. Your ads and marketing campaigns need to address products and services with the best price, best value and always have an added bonus.

Mary:

Generation X'ers (1965-1976)

Gen X'ers are not so easy to reach face-to-face. Gen X'er women are the highest viewers of home improvement media. They are averse to telemarketing and door-to-door solicitations. Traditional network TV struggles to reach this demographic. They are watchers of cable and internet for their shopping and entertainment. They do not respond to traditional advertising as much as they do to an irreverent approach. My first thought on this would be one of my personal favorites, "Flo" from Progressive Insurance. Instead of selling the features and benefits of the business, insurance companies have created cheeky characters to attract this generation to their firm.

When advertising, appear as the consultant rather than a seller of services. Short sound bites filled with information is preferable to them. The slick sale is a huge turnoff to the Gen X'ers. Leave your pitch at home! They appreciate an honest, straight-forward and factual approach.

Remember from our Buying Styles Answer Key, they don't like a lot of rules or commitments. It can prove useful to use this in your advertising efforts.

They make decisions together as a group; use this to your advantage. With today's global workforce, that group may not be located in one building. Emphasize your willingness to communicate using technology.

Strangely, they do respond to direct mail according to my research. Again, use the rules of advertising I suggested earlier in the design of your marketing pieces.

Ads need to be honest, family oriented, and unique to garner the attention of the Gen X'ers.

Generation Y's (1977-1990)

Creativity is vital with the Gen Y's. Companies must continually offer promotional themes to capture this audience. They respond to hype, not surprisingly when you combine the Buying Styles Answer Key information.

Ads are targeted to internet sites, phone apps, TV, video gaming, etc. A combination of online as well as offline advertising and marketing efforts works best. Word of mouth marketing is very important as peers influence their buying efforts. Social media dominates their lives. Focused efforts through Facebook pages, as one example, can draw the Gen Y's to you.

Music, language, and images are quite important in marketing efforts. Complacency is not in their dictionary. Stores need to regularly change their window dressings and displays to attract the Gen Y's. They get bored easily and will simply go elsewhere.

To approach the Gen Y's, use mobile marketing and social media to motivate them. They prefer a bit of humor or quirkiness, but always with the element of honesty.

YouTube is another channel to reach them. Humor is a way to show that you are not selling, nor taking yourself too seriously.

Contact them through their parents and grandparents as they are the Boomerang generation, and many Gen Y's do live at home. Do remember if you are targeting the Gen Y's parents, the avenues to reach them are different. Review the earlier part of this Answer Key.

They do watch TV, but prefer to DVR their shows and skip the commercials.

This generation is impatient. Information must be readily available to them. Social networking sites are important. Email is so yesterday to them; they prefer instant messaging, texting, and tweeting. Use of a landline phone is unlikely.

According to the Journal of Behavioral Studies in Business, your marketing effort should reach them digitally through:

- Websites
- Web Marketing
  - Electronic business cards (e-cards)
  - Banner advertisements
  - Pop-ups
  - Sponsorships
  - Content partnering
  - Screensavers
  - Desktop toys
- E-mail
- Online chat
- Webcasting
- Interactive television (Smart TV)
- Short message service (SMS) texts
- Wireless internet
- CD-ROMS/DVDs
- Digital radio

Content is critical for this generation; moving content from platform to platform with no restrictions is a must.

Green marketing is a powerful tool to get the attention of the Gen Y's. Green marketing has seen a strong growth rate because of this new phenomenon.

Generation Z's (born after 1990)

Marketers are increasingly targeting this segment. Gen Z's are influenced by new media, virtual friends, and the power that comes with technology. They have never lived without the internet and technology in some form or fashion.

It is not uncommon for them to use another form of media at the same time they are watching TV. With the use of Chatspeak, aka netspeak (example: u r gr8), their attention spans are shorter.

They have little tolerance for delays in customer service response times. This again has been driven by technology exposure and advances. If you wish to cater to this generation, your systems and people must be able to meet the needs of the Gen Z's. They are conditioned for speed.

Use of short videos, text marketing, and mobile ads that catch their eye is optimal. Social media marketing is another way to reach the Gen Z's.

Regularly update content and games. The Gen Z's operate on a fast pace and grow bored quickly, just like the Gen Y's, only faster.

With increased global terrorism, they have a need to feel safe. The recession has also had a significant influence in their need for security. They have witnessed much in their young lives. There are those who have also experienced the loss of a family member in war.

Since trust is so important to them, it is smart to begin a relationship early and continue to solidify and engage that relationship. Earning their trust now will have sticking power. Remember when trust has been violated, it is difficult, if not impossible, to get it back. Position your company as a customer-driven focused organization and live up to it!

Marketing messaging can remind them that, in a sometimes-scary world, they can still find positive people, organizations, and opportunities.

Mary's & Meredith's

Stories & Suggestions

Mary:

I see the generational differences creating perhaps the most confusion for the small business owners. Business owners are trying many channels, oftentimes without a strategy or follow-up plan. Frustration grows and marketing resources dwindle. An overall attitude change takes place as the marketing channel takes the blame for the failure when in fact it was a "spray and pray" attempt that was the breakdown.

This is when employees who have generational diversity, as well as allies in business, can help you. Mastermind and peer groups are also a great resource. Be careful of becoming almost addicted to every marketing seminar available. Over time these can end up confusing you with the differing approaches being presented. At the end of the day, someone standing at the front of the room proclaiming to be able to market your business, from the front of the room, doesn't know YOUR business. Get "face-to-face" with someone who is willing to understand your business from past, present, and future perspectives.

One additional suggestion, get a mobile friendly website because a significant amount of surfing the web now goes on using devices such as tablets and Smart Phones. Growing and shrinking screens becomes annoying after awhile. Having a mobile website can give you the edge on your competition and can make you more searchable online. Google loves mobile websites! It is not an expensive undertaking, and may be relatively easy to create for those who use a platform like Wordpress, or for do-it-yourselfers with available platforms and mobile friendly templates. Here are two samples of the same website, one mobile and one classic view. Which one would you prefer?

Meredith:

Every individual has five basic senses (touch, hearing, sight, smell, and taste). There is one other sense that often gets lost in our ads, and that is Common Sense. For the most part, most ads are only engaging in one or two senses at a time. The main ones are sight and sound. This strategy may work for some generations but not for all.

I know for some individuals the concept of engaging as many of the senses as possible becomes a determining factor for creating ads. Who can resist the new car smell or the aromas that come from entering a Yankee Candle store?

When facing the dilemma of what appeals to the generation you are focused on, taking time to look at all the various senses can be very illuminating. Studying the demographics of the various generations can give you clues to which senses dominate their lives and thus permeate their buying style.

As the Traditionalists and Boomers age, their senses also take a radical change. Ads that are busy or take too long to figure out what is being sold become a turn off to these people. Music that is too loud or contains language that a certain generation finds offensive can be a turn off. Generations' values can also be either promoted or belittled in an ad, and can be a detriment to getting a product or service sold.

The concept of Common Sense is often disregarded when ad campaigns are designed. This sense is very important to the Traditionalists and Boomers as they are foundational in who they are.

In any ad or marketing campaign, determining your market is the paramount goal. Combining a team of people who represent all the various targeted markets becomes fundamental in any advertising strategy. Give this team the goal of ascertaining which of the senses most appeals to the target audience.

If you structure your ad campaign in a way that addresses the primary senses of that generation, it will endear you and your product or service to that group. People of all generations want to be heard and listened to regarding their needs. When you engage their senses, they feel that you have connected to them on more than one level. A company or service that can create this involvement of the senses will always be a success.

This takes time; this takes the effort. This is advertising at its best when each individual's needs are addressed. This is the recipe for greatness for any marketing advertising campaign.

Application:

- Create a list of your marketing channels that you currently use.

- Create a list of the demographics by generation of your current customers.

- Apply the channels you currently use to the customer list.

  - Do they match?

  - Identify the gaps.

- What generations do you want your company to target in the future?

- Identify marketing channels that need to develop and create a timeline of implementation.

Discussion:

- Is there resistance to developing a new marketing strategy to reach your desired demographics more effectively?

  _____

  _____

  o Why?

  _____

  _____

- What business is being left on the table as a result of your marketing gaps?

  _____

  _____

  o In dollars?

  _____

  _____

- In customers/generations?

  _____

  _____

- Do you have the expertise currently to market to different generations?

  _____

  _____

- Are your products and services viable to the Gen Y's and Gen Z's?

  _____

  _____

- If not, what can your company do to appeal to these generations?

  _____

  _____

Answer Key Points

- Simply put... how people reach people. Who are the people you are trying to reach?

- Survey your market frequently.

- Channels need to match your customers and prospects.

- Marketing efforts need to be strategic and purposeful both in strategy and follow up.

- Using an impartial outside set of eyes with expertise in marketing can be invaluable to your business.

Answer Key 9

Values & Vision

Quotes:

Life's up and downs provide windows of opportunity to determine your values and goals. Think of using all obstacles as stepping stones to build the life you want. ~ _Marsha Sinetar_

It is easier to exemplify values than teach them. ~ _Theodore Hesburgh_

Values provide perspective in the best of times and worst.
~ _Charles A. Garfield_

Give to us clear vision that we may know where to stand and what to stand for because unless we stand for something, we shall fall for anything.
~ _Peter Marshall_

Meredith:

In our survey we asked the following question regarding what their vision of the future was at this time.

What statement best describes how you feel the world is heading?   Check only one.

☐ I am disappointed in the way things are going.

☐ I am not excited about where our world is heading.

☐ I feel that the world is a better place.

☐ I felt our generation was the best.

☐ I wish everyone would be more like our generation.

5 Generation Responses

	Trad.	Boomers	Gen X	Gen Y	Gen Z
Disappointed	1	10	7	1	
Not excited	2	20	7	2	
Better Place	1	10	4	2	1
Best Generation		1			
Be Like us					

Traditionalists (born prior to 1946)

Traditionalists feel they paid a great price for freedom. They are the generation in which love of country was their greatest value, next to God and family.

They have watched all this erode away, as nothing that they valued is held sacred anymore. They are disappointed and disillusioned that things appear like they are never going to get better. They feel that the good things in this world are gone, and it saddens them. They fought for ideals they believed in only to see those same ideals ridiculed and discarded.

They realize that the world is changing, and they do not have hope that the younger generation is going to make this world a better place. They see crippling debt in our economy, a flagrant disregard for the elderly, and realize that growing old is seen as a burden. Their wisdom is no longer valued or sought after.

They fear that these changes will result in programs and laws that will seek to eliminate them for being seen as a drain on the economy. The truth of the matter is they are the last generation that truly does have it together, both financially and as people of integrity. They were savers and didn't live beyond their means. Recessions and depressions only made them stronger. They had solid ground in their faith and their work ethics. They were the backbone of this country, and what made us strong were their values, hopes and dreams.

Boomers (born 1946-1964)

Boomers are predominately disillusioned, but there is still a strong contingent that is idealist and believes that everything is going to be alright.

I think this has to do with the two different groups comprising this segment. The older group is not confident that things are going to get better while the younger group feels that everything is going to be alright.

The truth of the matter is the old "half empty half full glass" mentality. If you think the world is going to fall apart, then things in your world will support it, and if you feel that there is a silver lining in every rain cloud, that is what you will get.

This group has had such dramatic upheavals in their lives; things that were amazing and some horrible yet they survived, and in some cases even thrived. They realized that not everything is black and white but definitely shades of gray. They realized that what they counted on for security could be eradicated in an instant, but they survived. Do they believe the next generation has this kind of fortitude? No way. Does that concern them? Oh yeah, because this next generation holds their future in their hands. Anyone who is not financially prepared for their future is headed for a rude awakening, and it is not pretty. This generation was a very definite "live now" generation when it came to their money and desires. Facing the future is frightening, and they see very little light at the end of the tunnel. Everywhere they turn there are things that create fear in their lives. They are too old to recover their financial losses and too healthy to die young. They hang on daily and do whatever is necessary to get by. They feel that they have been cheated. They paid their dues and played by the rules, but someone changed the game, and now they are at a loss what to do or where to go.

Mary:

Generation X'ers (1965-1976)

The Gen X'ers grew up in the shadows of the Boomers and watched as they gave their lives to work. As a result, this generation has watched families break up. They are the first generation to experience the complex issues relating to blended families. They have also witnessed the Boomers being downsized out of the corporate environment. Their values have been influenced by what has transpired around them. They do not live to work like their predecessors. They work to live. This defines their value system to the core. Their view of the world can be a little cynical and distrusting. Giving them the space to question will go a long way in building trust.

They do not see the value in spending long working hours in the workplace. They will perform at a higher level if given the flexibility to work but also to spend time in their personal lives. This can be a foreign concept to the generations preceding them because the mindset of those generations was based on work being a "sticks and bricks" environment with a desk/workspace to call their own. Gen X'ers have been raised, at some level, to appreciate technology and to see it as their way to achieve the work/life balance they value so dearly.

Gen X'ers also value the concept of fun. Workplaces

today are creating work environments that can offer their employees the resources to have fun. I have visited office buildings that have incorporated billiards, game tables, video games, as well as space design that incorporates the ability to be social and productive at the same time. Again, this is a foreign concept to the Boomers and Traditionalists. To the Gen X'ers, the need to have access to people is paramount. Isolation will simply demotivate them.

Their vision of what the world will look like is already taking shape in our workplace. Virtual offices, webinar meetings, telecommuting, etc. were nonexistent not all that long ago. As our Gen X'ers have become more numerous, and our Traditionalists have passed the torch, and the Boomers have begun to exit (forced or voluntary), the landscape is changing. With each passing year, the changes will continue...and not all that different from the pace that technology changes; this transition will gain momentum. It is a critical time in our workplace as the Gen X'ers move into roles of leadership. It will become increasingly difficult for companies to operate without investment into their people. In addition, the vision of where a company is going in 5, 10, and 20 years from now will need to be defined if companies want to survive and thrive. It will be necessary to incorporate the Gen X'ers in this process as they will be the leaders along with the Gen Y's and Gen Z's.

Generation Y's (1977-1990)

Gen Y's value your skills and ability, not your status in society or the workplace. No longer can one ride on their laurels or success stories from long ago. Command and control will not work for them. They have not lived under those rules or methods in their homes or schools.

Gen Y's are achievement oriented... let me explain, they have a greater focus on their future goals and potential. They have high expectations of their employers, are willing to seek out new challenges, and are not shy about questioning authority. They just don't put a lot of value in anything that does not move them closer to their goals.

They are family-centric and are willing to trade higher pay for a work/life balance. It is not uncommon for Gen Y's to be labeled as narcissistic or as lacking commitment or drive, but they have a different vision of the workplace expectations and priorities.

They have been raised in environments where parents fawned over them. They do crave attention. That can be viewed in two ways – **DIFFERENT, therefore WRONG, or NOT WRONG, just DIFFERENT**. If someone who craves attention does not get positive attention, they often will seek negative attention. Creating an environment of mentorship can go a long way in providing the attention the Gen Y's need as well as providing mentoring opportunities for those generations preceding the Gen Y's.

Gen Y's have a need to understand what they will contribute in the overall vision. They will be good strategic leaders in our future, being team oriented and vision focused – two excellent qualities of a great leader. They do not see themselves as just another spoke in the wheel. While preceding generations cannot often see how their job fits into the puzzle, the Gen Y's absolutely see the puzzle as a whole.

Gen Y's ask Why. This may be a cool way to identify if you have a Gen Y thinker in front of you. Why do they ask why? When they ask questions, they are not met with the typical "I told you so" or because "I'm the boss" response like Boomers were. Questions presented teaching opportunities for the Gen Y's parents. It is not a fear or punishment inducing question; it is an opportunity to learn! This may be one of those big "Aha" moments for many who are reading this book. Take the extra 30 seconds to explain why to the Gen Y's, and they will have a greater chance at meeting your expectations.

Generation Z's (born after 1990)

Gen Z's value transparency. Their lives are an open book. Clearly, social media has opened the door for this behavior. They are a very ethnically diverse generation as well. They have exposure to global information and have it 24/7. They thrive on LIVE community – which to them can be global.

They are self-reliant. Technology has played a huge role in this. Their home and school lives have also influenced this. Their lives have been streamlined and technology assisted. It is interesting that advertising is now using a humorous approach to convey this very message.

They must have flexibility. Their lives have been defined by this. School curriculums have incorporated this into their lives as well. Rigid hours and agendas are foreign to them. Their minds operate at higher speed and multi-task. We may not understand it; nevertheless, it is a way of life for them.

They don't really care about fame and fortune. They care more about making a difference. They care about their environment, their community, and global humanitarian issues. These values are important to them to the point that they will choose employers based on their passions and efforts in these areas. The influences of global terrorism have had an influence, but at the same time, their exposure to global news has also played a part.

They are pessimistic about the future. It is no wonder with the economic problems they have experienced since a young age. They have constant access to information and are well informed of global issues. They have watched their families go from wealth to poverty with the recession. Homelessness of families affected our nation as a whole, and it was all over the news. I can recall a story where bus routes included low cost motels so that kids in Kissimmee Florida could be picked up; a high number of families had lost their homes due to the economic collapse. This was just one example of many that this generation experienced on a very personal level.

With all this being said, the Gen Z's are still in development. The longer our economic struggles continue, the more impact it will have on them. This is similar to our Traditionalists and the Great Depression. There is much research that indicates that Gen Y's will begin to circle back around and adopt values similar to the Traditionalists. Time will tell. One thing we know for sure is that by 2020 the workplace will change dramatically as the Gen Y's and Gen Z's take their place as the majority in the workplace. I will reinforce the necessity for companies to prepare and invest now into planning what your long-term BHAG (Big Hairy

Audacious Goals) are for your future. Where is your company at currently in moving towards those goals, and do you have the people in place to get you there?

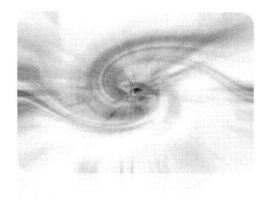

Mary's & Meredith's

Stories & Suggestions

Mary:

As we indicated early on in this book in the Introduction, values are based upon our life's influences and the experiences from those close to us, as well as our political and global events. Values are extremely unique and personal to the individual. In my experience, personality dimensions do influence, to some degree, whether someone will defend their values or share their visions. The reality is we all have them; just because someone is not willing to verbally defend their values or visions, doesn't mean they are not important to them. People will defend their values in many ways. Recall when Meredith was defining Communication Verbal & Nonverbal? Disengagement of employees can be statements they make when their values are pinched or disrespected. It can also be a sign that their vision of the company is skewed from what the true vision is.

What can you do Mr. or Ms. Business Owner/Leader/ Manager?

- Own your own vision and values, both personally and professionally.
- Understand the values and vision of each employee.
- Find the commonalities and build upon those.

If values are violated, there are consequences to all involved. Be willing to own these if they are your actions that were involved in the event. Take action to effectively address the issue.

Your vision of the company may also be limited to just your generational view. Acknowledge this and create a best thinking/consensus building environment where your teams can openly share their visions and ideas without fear of contempt or criticism.

Companies I see utilize these ideas thrive in the market and have BHAGs that are taking shape one day at a time.

Meredith:

I am who I am because of my values. You are who you are because of your values. I may not agree with your values, and you may not agree with mine, but agreeing or disagreeing should never be the foundation of the respect we have for each other.

Each generation has developed a set of values, and sometimes the differences are as wide as the Grand Canyon. Even though that may be the case, respect for our different values is imperative if a business is to succeed and thrive.

Every company or service needs to have core values at the center. These core values then permeate that company, and anyone working for or with that company needs to share those values. There are certain common values that cross all generational lines. These are the values that become the easiest to adhere to.

As a company leader, do your employees share those core values? Have you even shared them, and if not, is it because they are things you think everyone already knows? It always amazes me how often people assume things and then judge people when they fail to live up to their standards.

When you determine your core values, what are the nonnegotiable vs. negotiable ones? Often we cherish a value that may not be commonly shared. How important is that value to you and your company? Are you willing to compromise? I recently read the core values of Hobby Lobby and Chick-fil-A, and one of their core values is God and family. Both of these companies feel so strongly about this particular core value that they are not open on Sundays. This was a huge stand for what they believed in, as Sundays are considered one of the busiest for fast food and retail. Yet both companies refused to budge on upholding their core values.

Values are important and are determined by many factors in one's life.

How do your core values show up in your workplace? Are you willing to take a stand for them, or are they just nice platitudes on a plaque in the foyer of your building?

Application:

- Write down your core values.

- Ask your core leadership and management groups to write down their values.

- Request your employees to submit their values as well.

- Compare results.

  o Identify commonalities
  o Identify differences

- Repeat above steps but use Vision statements.

Discussion:

- What are your core values as it relates to:

  o Business?

  _____

  _____

  o Finance?

  _____

  _____

  o Personal?

  _____

  _____

- What are the events in your life that have had the greatest impact on you?

  _____

  _____

    o   Why?

_____

_____

- Who are the people who have had the greatest influence in your life?

- Closest to you (family, clergy, educators, etc.)

_____

_____

    o   Why?

_____

_____

- In the media (politics, entertainment, etc.)

_____

_____

    o   Why?

_____

_____

- What is your vision of your company if you are an owner?

  _____

  _____

- What is the vision of your career, if you are an owner or an employee?

  _____

  _____

- What events have changed that vision in the past?

  _____

  _____

  - Why?

    _____

    _____

- What events have changed that vision recently?

  _____

  _____

o Why?

_____

_____

• If you are an owner, who can you include for developing your Mission, Vision, Values and Purpose statements?

_____

_____

o Why?

_____

_____

Answer Key Points

- Gen Y's ask Why.

- Vision and Values are personal and unique to every person.

- People will defend their values as they know them.

- Build upon commonalities.

- Build an environment where Best Thinking is a common practice in planning, problem solving, and conflict resolution.

Answer Key 10

Passing the Torch

Quotes:

Tell me what are the prevailing sentiments that occupy the minds of your young men, and I will tell you what is to be the character of the next generation. ~ Edmund Burke

We will have to repent in this generation not merely for the hateful words and actions of the bad people but for the appalling silence of the good people. ~ Martin Luther King, Jr.

We need to teach the next generation of children from day one that they are responsible for their lives. Mankind's greatest gift, also its greatest curse, is that we have free choice. We can make our choices built from love or from fear. ~ Elisabeth Kubler-Ross

Meredith:

In our survey we asked the following question regarding passing the torch.

What statement best describes how you feel about passing the torch?   Check only one.

☐ I want the next generation to do better than I did.

☐ I want the next generation to follow my lead.

☐ I want the next generation to learn from my mistakes.

☐ I want the next generation to follow their own way.

5 Generation Responses

	Trad.	Boomers	Gen X	Gen Y	Gen Z
Do Better	2	20	13	3	1
Follow my lead		3	1		
Learn from mistakes	1	10	2	3	
Follow own way	1	11	2		

Traditionalists (born prior to 1946)

When questioning the Traditionalists about what they wanted to leave as their legacy, they mainly fell into one of two camps and they are:

I want the next generation to do better than I did.

I want the next generation to learn from my mistakes.

Interesting that this greatest generation did not feel that they were able to figure out what was the best. I think part of that was a humility that came with this generation. They did not have an entitlement mentality; they worked for everything they got. They did not want to keep up with the neighbors because their values were rich in past history. They lived life to the fullest giving 100% to whatever they did. They expected honesty and integrity from the people in their world, and they were willing to give it to those they encountered. Their handshake was their bond, and they were not concerned about contracts and lawsuits. They felt an honest day's work for an honest wage determined the value of a person. They valued family and believed that people should strive to always become better. They expected honesty from others and sought ways to be honest with them.

They believed they lived in the greatest country and felt it was worth dying for. They took people at face value, and not until proven otherwise did they change. They believed a person innocent until proven guilty, and that the measure of a man was his word.

They believed that there was always room for improvement, and they were not prideful enough to think they knew everything.

They realized that they had made mistakes and hoped that future generations would learn from them.

Boomers (born 1946-1964)

Boomers, when asked about their legacy, separated in three different camps. Two of them were similar to the Traditionalists, but they differed on a third.

I want the next generation to do better than I did.

I want the next generation to learn from my mistakes.

I want the next generation to follow their own way.

This divergence is the most telling because the Boomers were the generation that did exactly that. They were the radicals. They were the ones that protested a war that they could not believe in. They fought for things that their parents accepted. They sought ways to improve society and the world at large. They were not willing to settle, and they wanted everyone to find their own path.

Their legacy started a revolution of change. Some good and some not so good, but they chose not to judge. It was all about change. If ideals were trampled and values destroyed, so be it. They were the proverbial "throwing out the baby with the bathwater" in the things that they did. Change was their mantra, and change they did. The world is still rocking from the changes that became manifested by this generation. Some changes were simply acts of rebellion, and some changes were actually for the betterment of mankind. The sad factor on this generation is that they failed to really look at an end vision, and instead focused on the here and now. The reason for this is they didn't have an end vision.

Mary:

Generation X'ers (1965-1976)

Research shows that a key factor in the generations after the Boomers is that they are unwilling to work the long hours that Boomers and Traditionalists have sacrificed for decades.

The Gen X'ers are willing to confront management and leadership styles that, in their view, are archaic. They will leave their own mark on companies going forward.

It will be necessary to integrate the wisdom of the past with the innovations that Gen X'ers see for the future. This is a critical reason to bring expertise into an organization's succession planning, and to bring it in long before hands change.

Some of the critical challenges in transitioning Gen X'ers to ownership are:

- Blunt communication styles and the leadership challenge

- Work/Life balance and what it means to the X'er vs. the Boomer

- Helping the Gen X'ers in their impatience and moving them to a more patient and strategic long-term view of the future

In family businesses, never assume that the next generation even wants the torch. They have witnessed much during the generations preceding them. They are educated and technology aware. What you expect for the future business may not be what they see as their future. Open communication is necessary, along with preparation, in advance of any transition.

For many business owners, passing the torch may be the sale of the business and passing on the financial assets.

Generation Y's (1977-1990)

Transparency, transparency, transparency! Gen Y's have a need to understand the process as well as their own role within that process. Traditionalists and Boomers have been known to keep things "close to the vest" in their companies. This only serves to frustrate the Gen Y's. Remember, they are not loyal to one company. Creating this type of closed environment only supports their initiative to leave.

Some of the challenges the preceding generations create for the Gen Y's are:

- Withholding information about employees' potential. If you have a Gen Y who possesses high potential, tell them so. Invest in their development. Create an environment that promotes their staying power.

- Excluding them from the process can cost you their motivation, participation, and insights into the future. Keep your Gen Y's engaged in the process.

- "Too busy" to communicate progress, gratitude, and results? Feedback must be prompt and thorough at all times. Don't forget, Gen Y's ask Why; be prepared to seize the opportunities to mentor.

Gen Y's have a wider view of the world; support that by sharing the strategic aspects of the succession plan. Help them understand what part they play.

Gen Y's will impact the business world because they have been raised in a tech savvy way. Re-read the Answer Keys on Leadership, Technology, Work Ethic, etc. to get a handle on what the future looks like when the Gen Y's are in control. For them, the office is not so much brick and mortar, but just an extension of their personal lives.

Generation Z's (born after 1990)

It may be difficult to get your arms around a Gen Z running the company. They will be few and far between for awhile. They are entrepreneurial and have created successful organizations in areas that they have cornered the market in, such as social media management, technology (especially apps for phones, tablets, etc.) and the like.

There is not much data out there relating to Gen Z's passing the torch. As we go forward, consider the qualities that were listed for Gen Z's in the introduction of this book.

Gen Z's are more confident, better educated, faster thinkers, open to change and innovation, and technology dependent.

Managers will not boss; they will coach. Leaders will be authentic and focused on more than the company's success. Global landscape and sustainability will be integrated within the purpose of the company.

Companies will be 24/7 through the use of technology, and this exists today in many sectors of industry. "Brick and mortar" offices will be much more optional, meaning that the workforce may not all live within nearby zip codes.

Mary's & Meredith's

Stories & Suggestions

Mary:

I have had several conversations recently with a variety of business allies about succession planning. It is true that many businesses are transitioning from the Traditionalists and older Boomers. Many of these are family businesses, and they are running into some significant changeover issues. Many of the concerns are at the heart of why we wrote this book in the first place. Businesses operate on the conventional wisdom, "it has worked for us to this point, why change the mindset now." Another position might be to just let the new regime deal with the necessary updates to the company. At this point, the transfer of the business can be difficult as well as the recovery after the transfer. As it is, business success after a merger or acquisition can be dicey if we only just consider the impact to customers and existing employees. Generational factors can add layers of issues that may bring a business to the brink of failure. It is mission critical to employ a team of experts to help in an organization's process of passing the torch.

Additionally, there are many young business owners who are involved in the merger and acquisition process. With the emergence of technology, many young entrepreneurs have created successful and thriving companies that are positioned to be acquired by larger firms or purchased by other entrepreneurs. The dynamics of the generations in such purchases can look very different. Bringing those businesses to market and communicating with prospective buyer/owners has also taken on a different approach considering the internet and digital media.

The face of business will look quite different by 2020 according to statistics. That is just a short 6 years from now (as of the writing of this book). If you wish to sell or pass down your business, the time is now for beginning the process.

Meredith:

You created your business. You worked tirelessly to make it a success. In some cases you sacrificed your family and health, all in the name of making sure your business succeeded.

Now it looks like someone else will be at the helm. They will make the decisions. Depending on which generation you are coming from, the idea of someone else taking over can be downright scary. Maybe you were fortunate enough to have a son or daughter that you groomed to take over, and they have the same passion to continue, or maybe they don't. Maybe it will be strangers who buy your company. I think the younger generations find it easier to sell a business they have created because they feel they can go out and create another one. On the other hand, the older generations (Traditionalists and Boomers) feel that once their company is gone, so is a part of their lives. They are not the optimists who think they will go out and create another company. They know what it took to create the first one, and the thought of doing that again is daunting.

If you are in a position to take over a company, keep the differences in mind. To one generation, you are taking their child; to another, you are taking an idea that they were able to create.

Application:

- What stage are you currently at in your succession planning process?

- Write down key members of your team.

- Create a list of potential successors to your business.

- What generations do they belong to – review the Introduction?

- What qualities, values, and preferences do they have from other generations?

- Develop goals to begin / execute / complete your process of Passing the Torch.

Discussion:

- What alternatives does your company have in succession planning?

  _____

  _____

- Consider these and write comments down, discuss with shareholder/leadership team:

  o Transfer the business to current shareholders from generations younger than you.

  _____

  _____

  o Sell the business to a new owner:

  _____

  _____

o Sell the business to a larger company as a merger.

_____

_____

o Dissolve the business and invest any remaining assets.

_____

_____

o Sell the business earlier than your expected retirement, and continue to work in the business on your own terms.

_____

_____

o Continue ownership of the business, but transfer leadership and management to others.

_____

_____

- What next steps are required to begin your succession planning process?

_____

_____

- Who are critical professionals outside your company that you will need?

  _____

  _____

- Do you have relationships? If not, who can you turn to for referrals?

  _____

  _____

Answer Key Points

- It is easy to get into business; it can be difficult to get out of business without proper planning.

- Succession planning involves the input and inclusion of key people from several generations in your organization.

- What your company looks like today will most definitely be quite different from what it looks like tomorrow.

- The earlier you invest in planning, the greater the benefit can be to you and your organization.

What is the Next Generation?

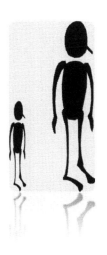

Quotes about our youth:

Youth lives on hope, old age on memories. ~ <u>Proverb</u>

The young do not know enough to be prudent, and therefore they attempt the impossible -- and achieve it, generation after generation.
~ <u>Pearl Buck</u>

There is always one moment in childhood when the door opens and lets the future in. ~ <u>Deepak Chopra</u>

Let's tell young people the best books are yet to written; the best painting, the best government, the best of everything is yet to be done by them.
~ <u>John Erskine</u>

Generation Alpha....but of course!

Our Generation Alpha's are born after 2003. They have been raised by Gen X'ers and Gen Y's.

Predicted to:

- Be the largest generation to date
- Adopt technology faster (hard to believe that is even possible)
- Have increased health concerns (hmmmm …read on for the answer to this one)
- Start earlier and stay longer in school
- Have better career opportunities due to a skills shortage, created by the present population leaving the workforce

Why health concerns?

Because of the lack of exercise and the food they eat.

Exercise is lacking due to severe cuts in education budgets, as well as the lifestyle this generation, and the Gen Y's and Gen Z's, have lived. Health challenges, typical of older people, will be experienced at much younger ages due to the sedentary lifestyle.

Diet issues because the food we eat has changed. This is a hot topic currently, and I perceive will continue to be for years to come. Foods are being imported from other countries that have different standards regarding pest control and what they feed the livestock and such, and the chemicals that are added to the foods. In addition, food, like technology, has become "faster." And finally, genetically modified food has taken our country by storm.

FYI – the young boy by the fountain in the picture is Mary's very own Gen Alpha, her grandson – Noah. The children in the lower computer picture are Meredith's grandchildren Alyza and Wyatt, also Alpha's.

With all of this new awareness of generational diversity, we leave you with one additional question...

What can you do today to make a positive impact on Generation Alpha through your behavior modeling, knowledge, expertise, and mentorship?

Survey Questions

"10 Answer Keys, Communicating with the 5 Generations in the Workplace"

When were you born?

- ☐ prior to 1946
- ☐ 1946-1964
- ☐ 1965-1976
- ☐ 1977-1990
- ☐ born after 1990

Are you?

- ☐ Male
- ☐ Female

What statement best describes your favorite type of communication?   Check only one.

- ☐ Email
- ☐ Face to Face
- ☐ Letter
- ☐ Phone call
- ☐ Text

What statement best describes your work ethic? Check only one.

- ☐ Cluttered but know where everything is
- ☐ Organized
- ☐ Cluttered but my secretary knows where everything is
- ☐ Job must be done
- ☐ Job must be done right

What statement best describes your time management? Check only one.

- ☐ Always late
- ☐ Fashionably late most of the time
- ☐ Late occasionally
- ☐ Never late

What statement best describes your first response when you are upset? Check only one.

- ☐ Angry words face-to-face
- ☐ Blast them on Facebook
- ☐ Silent treatment/ignore them
- ☐ Text them your feelings
- ☐ Write them a letter

What statement best describes your management and leadership style? Check only one.

- ☐ I am the boss.
- ☐ I don't strive to lead.
- ☐ I follow my own lead no matter who is in charge.
- ☐ I follow whoever is in charge.
- ☐ I take charge when I realize there is a lack of leadership.

What statement best describes how you get your information? Check only one.

- ☐ I get my information from my friends.
- ☐ I get my information from the print (newspaper, books, and articles).
- ☐ I get my information from the web.
- ☐ I get my information from TV, radio.
- ☐ I get my information through research from a multitude of sources.

What statement best describes your feelings about technology? Check only one.

- ☐ I am comfortable with technology.
- ☐ I came kicking and screaming into technology, but now I am ok.
- ☐ I love technology.
- ☐ I tolerate technology.
- ☐ I understand technology most of the time.

What statement best describes your buying styles? Check only one.

- [ ] I do my shopping online – Amazon, Online stores, etc.
- [ ] I look for bartering or exchanges, Craigslist, eBay.
- [ ] I shop where I have no one bothering me.
- [ ] I would prefer face-to-face sales.

Which statement best describes how you want someone to sell you something?   Check only one.

- [ ] I hate advertising.
- [ ] I love to read ads in newspapers, magazines.
- [ ] I prefer face to face advertising.
- [ ] I tolerate ads on TV.

What statement best describes how you feel the world is heading?   Check only one.

- [ ] I am disappointed in the way things are going.
- [ ] I am not excited about where our world is heading.
- [ ] I feel that the world is a better place.
- [ ] I felt our generation was the best.
- [ ] I wish everyone would be more like our generation.

What statement best describes how you feel about passing the torch?   Check only one.

☐   I want the next generation to do better than I did.
☐   I want the next generation to follow my lead.
☐   I want the next generation to learn from my mistakes.
☐   I want the next generation to follow their own way.

Email your completed survey to:

Meredith@MeredithBromfield.com

Contributors & References:

Alexandra Glumac, MS, NCC, LCPC, RDDP, "Dealing with Difficult Personalities at Work and Diffusing Hostile Customers"

"Tips for Managing Five Different Generations at Work," www.managingyourhr.com/five-generations

"Wikipedia,The Free Encyclopedia," http://en.wikipedia.org/wiki/Main_Page

Benjamin Spock, "Discipline Overview," website article, available at www.DrSpock.com

"Working With Five Generations In The Workplace," www.forbes.com

"Recruiting in The Five Generation Workplace" by Jessica Miller-Merrell

"Five Steps to Bridging the Workplace Generation Gap," Carebridge Corporation, www.princeton.edu

"Are You Ready to Manage Five Generations of Workers?" by Neanne C. Meister and Karie Willyerd, *Harvard Business Review*

"Traditionalists, Baby Boomers, Generation X, Generation Y (and Generation Z) Working Together" by United Nations Joint Staff Pension Fund

"Traditionalists, Boomers, Xers, and Millennial Giving and Getting the Mentoring You Want,"
Cathy A. Trowner, Ph.D., Brown University

"The Traditional Generation [Born 1922–1945]," www.valueoptions.com

"Meet the Generations," www.missouri.edu

"The Baby Boomer Generation [Born 1946–1964]," www.valueoptions.com

"Generation X" by Sally Kane, www.about.com

"Generation X and The Millennials: What You Need to Know About Mentoring the New Generations" by Diane Thielfoldt and Devon Scheef

"Millennials, Gen Y, Gen X — Can't we all get along?" by Kathy McCarron

"Guide to Recent U.S. "Generations," United States Popular Culture Reference File

"America's Gen Y," www.metlife.com

"Is Gen Y Becoming the New Lost Generation?" by Ray B. Williams, www.psychologytoday.com

"Generation Y" by Sally Kane

"5 Key Characteristics of Generation Y" by Nicole Fougere

"Multigenerational Characteristics" by Burce Mayhew Consulting

"Marketing to Gen Y: What you can't afford not to know" by Bea Fields

"Generation Z as Consumers: Trends and Innovation" by Stacy Wood

"Generation Z: A Look at the Technology and Media Habits of Today's Teens," www.wikia.com

"3 Ways Companies Can Reach Generation Z," www.mashable.com

"Consumers of Tomorrow Insights and Observations About Generation Z" by Grail Research

"How Generation Z Works" by Lance Looper

"Marketing across the Generations," www.marketingcharts.com

"Generations X, Y, Z and the Others" by William J. Schroer

"Power of Generation Marketing" by Laura Lake

"Defining, Managing, and Marketing to Generations X, Y, and Z" by The Portal

"Marketing for the Generations" by Jennifer Neeley Lindsay

"Understanding the Technological Generation Gap" by Larry D. Rosen, Ph.D.

"Generations + Technology" by Bernardo Tirado

"Succession Planning: Raising Up the Next Generation of Leaders" by Kurt R. Podeszwa

"Family business succession planning for the lost generation" by Patricia Annino

"Involve the younger generations in succession planning" by Phyllis Weiss Haserot

"Why Millennials Are Ditching Cars and Redefining Owner" by Noah Nelson

"Marketing to the Generations" by Kaylene C Williams and Robert A. Page

Survey Participants:

We sincerely thank everyone for sharing their insights on **Communicating with the 5 Generations in the Workplace**. We appreciate you taking the time to help.

Jim Kelderhouse, Donald Curby, John Mailander, Eric Van Ness, Gene Knapp, Jason Thalman, John Noyes, Jennifer Piazza, Dan Baeten, Jim Mayo, Brandy Harrington, Dee Reinhardt, Skip Marshall, Paul Feith, Namisha Patel, Michael Ochs, Tony Hotko, Keith French, Alexandra Glumac, Karen Andrews, Jerry Grable, Mike Peters, Glenn Turner, Paul Stevenson, Don Jones, Leen Ghandour Hillas, Debbie Bertram, Kurt Niederpruem, Jim Martin, Dante Royster, Janice Ilg, Sandy Gilbert, Elizabeth Londo, Michelle Binks, Scott Langford, Bobi Siembieda, Shirley Fancher, Kent Vincent, Vic Portillo, Kanan Desai, Pete Gilfillan, Tom Bennington, Bryan Headley, Michael Field, Don Sinnott, Karen Shabel, John Koranda, Robin Wilson, Andy Krivograd, Lilly Gaspar, Sharon Case, Lou Costabile, Frank Blood, Donna Costabile, Phyllis Rosano, Tod Petrie, Jack Beuse, Nancy Brunetti, Roberta Brunner, Suzy Cameron West, Geoffrey Carreiro, Katie Conrad,

Norma Diaz, Nancy Ekdahl, Kathy Grames, Pat Grandle, Barbara Harris, Doug Kelley, Ruth LaVigne, Lynne Manzer, Jim Mayo, Juliana Naddy Smith, John Pineman, Ken Schmidt, Linda Serafini, Gary Summers, J.W. Sykes, Marilyn Tappy, Helen Williams, Stephanie Ludeman, Jim Cudney, Tom Ruby, Wendy Edwards, Holly Keenon, Cynthia Warsaw, Deb Baker, Greg Woodard, Libby Paul, Mike Jackson, Tiffany Anderson, Darwin Mintu, Gail Sanecki, Donna Scariti, Albert Sunserl, Thomas Nanninga, Kim Shannon, Jon, Llaguno, Lori Grana, Andrea Trovato, Jim Gardner, Larry DeLegge, Steve Geslak, Debbie Gregorash, Joe Gillespie, Joel Regier, Bob Riffner, Danielle Girdano, Alan Lee, Tom Hansen, Butch Zemar, Donna Schroeppel, William Wenk, Kent Vincent, Rich Brown, Roberta Williamson, Tom Votrain, Brandon Walton, Gary Summers, Randy Stadtfeld, Beth Propst, Jonathan Nohe, Dan Menis, Ruth-Ann McKellin, Harry McCabe, Lyne Manzer, Mary Malinowski, Kim Lien Pham, John Leone, Jake Korgleis, Thomas Kozlowski, Doug Kelley, Phyllis Hoffman, Jean Harris, Barbara Harris, Jody Hargett, Edward Hardt, Sr., Joe Garlin, Michelle Farra, Henry Farnd, Mary Bolin

If we have missed anyone, we sincerely apologize. If we have misspelled the names in any way, please give us some grace. Many people gave us survey results but wished to remain anonymous. We sincerely thank all participants for sharing their survey answers with us.

Mary Erlain

I am the founder and President of Peak Development Strategies, a business coaching and professional development firm. I co-facilitate the Entrepreneurs Groups and the Managers Groups in the Chicagoland area. I am proud to be a certified associate of Leadership Management® International, Inc., and am a certified sales auditor / Director of training and development with Verde Martin, Inc. I have co-authored books and am a sought after professional speaker on business topics.

I believe the best way to reenergize a business owner and their business is to develop a personalized plan strong enough to overcome any issues. With candor, encouragement and insight, my passion is to address the needs of people in business in a learning style that is comfortable for them. I also have been given a gift of connecting people. I am a valued referral source for my alliance partners and will continue to use this gift to benefit others. I truly live by the "give first" principle in business and have used that as the cornerstone in building my business. I know what my boundaries are as a coach and seek to collaborate with others to help my clients. I created my organization to help people in "Connecting the dots and removing barriers! ™"

My mission in life is to complete my life's journey knowing that I helped as many people as possible to develop themselves and discover their God-given gifts and talents. In my business, I use the tools that I have, and continue to learn, to coach, and develop people.

I have a very special story to share with people that is an example of how God can work miracles in people's lives. My experiences in life did not happen just for me to own all by myself; instead, they will be shared with others as sources of hope.

Only by Grace,

Mary

You can contact me by e-mail:

M.Erlain@Peak-DS.com

Please also visit these websites:

www.Peak-DS.com

www.LinkedInWorkshops.com

Meredith "Kit" Bromfield

I am transformation strategist. I help people change. My experience as an investment advisor, author, advocate, inspirational speaker, and founder of Crossing Your Bridge are all designed to aid in that process.

My passion is to make a difference in the lives of the people I come in contact with. Who I am, what I do, and what I have created in a Company is all about making people feel special and giving them choices when they are facing a life-changing event, whether the event is aging, becoming a caregiver, divorce, employment issues or finances.

I have designed programs to offer hope-filled solutions through coaching, workshops, books, and weekly "Words of Wisdom."

My desire is to empower you to live your life with purpose, passion, and prosperity. Through personal guidance and a multitude of resources, I will help you explore options to help you customize solutions for "crossing your bridge." No matter what "bridge" you are facing, there are keys that will help ease your journey.

With a Grateful Heart,

Meredith

You can contact me by e-mail:

Meredith@MeredithBromfield.com

Please also visit these websites:

www.MeredithBromfield.com

www.CrossingYourBridge.com